# THE MASTER'S TOUCH

*Treasures in Earthen Vessels*

**JOYCE ROBINSON**

Trilogy Christian Publishers

A Wholly Owned Subsidary of Trinity Broadcasting Network

2442 Michelle Drive

Tustin, CA 92780

For information, address Trilogy Christian Publishing

Rights Department, 2442 Michelle Drive, Tustin, CA 92780.

Trilogy Christian Publishing/TBN and colophon are trademarks of Trinity Broadcasting Network.

For information about special discounts for bulk purchases, please contact Trilogy Christian Publishing.

Manufactured in the United States of America

10 9 8 7 6 5 4 3 2 1

Library of Congress Cataloging-in-Publication Data is available.

ISBN 979-8-89041-111-2

ISBN (ebook) 979-8-89041-112-9

# FOREWORD

*Poetry has been defined as "the measured language of emotion," something possessing beauty, intensity and truth. God used poetry all throughout the Bible to reach hearts over thousands of years. When we read poems, we are transported through the words of the poet, sharing life experiences and wisdom. And when Joyce Robinson is the poet behind the pen, you know you will always be in for a beautiful journey. She has a masterful way of tying together Biblical truths with life lessons, leaving you yearning for more. This is no surprise as she has been a "nail in a sure place" (Isaiah 22:23) to her church for over 45 years. Gifted by God, Joyce is a prolific writer and this newest volume is sure to touch your heart and speak to your soul.*

- Bishop Dan Willis,
Founder & Bishop of The Lighthouse
Church of All Nations, Alsip, IL

# TABLE OF CONTENTS

# THE BATTLE IS
# THE LORD'S

# AT HIS FEET

People in Bible days heard about the power of the Lord.
They gathered their sick as their hopes soared.
Just to get their loved one whole and complete,
Great efforts were made to cast them at His feet.

Mary Magdalene, undesired by the community,
Rejected and unloved, she suffered humility.
Knelt before the Savior, feeling like sifted wheat,
Found complete forgiveness, weeping at His feet.

Legion raved through the tombs of the dead,
A man that was avoided with great dread.
A word spoken by Jesus made him complete,
Found with a right mind, learning at His feet.

As one steps in His courts and bows before His throne,
He reaches forth His hand when praises are known.
Unworthy and humbly this majestic God meet,
He bestows an overwhelming mercy at His feet.

Our lives for Him may seem to waver,
But there is only hope in our blessed Savior.
We sometimes find ourselves in defeat,
But there is power and victory at His feet.

# CHAMPION IN CHAINS

A servant, obedient, with singleness of heart,
Having a shield of faith, quenching Satan's fiery dart.
Not with eye service, but a passion of desire
Strong in the Lord, tested by His fire.
A Champion raising God's banner unfurled,
Standing against the wickedness of the world.

Working diligently, he takes pride in his tasks,
Daily prayer forgotten, a chain unnoticed clasp.
No devotion, forgetting truth, his visions dissipate.
Anger sets in, turns to bitterness and hate.
His feet running without peace when once was shod
This Champion quickly loses the armor of God.

The precious helmet of Salvation is lost in the fight.
Losing the battle, God's no longer his might.
Doubt enters, losing faith as his shield.
Another chain clings, the Champion lies in the field,
Chains wrapped around him unaware of sin.
Trapped helplessly, he realizes the state he's in.

Through prayer and supplication, God breaks the chain.
Picks up the wounded soul and heals the pain.
We wrestle not against flesh, but principalities and powers.
Oh! That we could learn the battle is not ours.
For God gives us armor and power to stand
If we learn to completely trust and follow His command.

# DEVELOPING THE NEGATIVE

In the beginning, God had a picture in His mind
Let's make in our "image" all of mankind.
Satan wanted his debut in this great endeavor,
So, he devised a plan that he thought was clever.

The picture was beautiful and without blemish
When everything in God's creation was finished.
But Satan was there to introduce the first sin.
So, God had to redesign His work from within.

We read how Aaron the high priest lied about the steer.
Moses, in anger, killed an Egyptian and fled in fear.
Jacob deceived his brother for the birthright blessing,
Paul breathed out death threats of Christians confessing.

It looked like the perfect picture was ruined at best,
But God was taking the negative through the test.
It's the dark places that He puts His creation through
In the dark room developing the negative anew.

When we're going through something we don't understand,
We're just being dipped in the solution by His mighty hand.
The process of the dipping and dark room of what we can't see,
Is just God developing the negative for the picture He wants to be.

Time seems to linger, and we wonder why the test or trial.
He is perfecting our hearts and lives all the while.
We shall come forth "in His image," in the picture of His plans
If we are willing to go through the darkroom as He commands.

# FOUNTAIN EVERLASTING

There are souls all around us groping in the night,
Wandering aimlessly, knowing not their plight.
So confused to escape from the wilderness they are in,
Needing a drink of Life to free them from sin.

We may have trials that take us through the flame
With all the problems which come again and again.
Oh, weary ones that trudge along your way.
There's a place of abundant refreshing for you today!

A wounded, hurting heart may seem to linger on
A heaviness hovers stealing your song.
Bring your burden to Jesus and then
Let the healing waters mend your heart again.

Fountain Everlasting flowing for every kindred and nation,
Satisfying every soul with healing and salvation.
Fountain Everlasting, send Your anointing today,
Send Your Holy Spirit in the old-time way.

# FRAGMENTS

After teaching throughout the day, Jesus gave the command:
Sit the people down, only He knew His awesome plan,
In companies of fifty arrange all the men
Women and children were situated, and then

Jesus said to His disciples, His voice loud and clear,
"We can't send these hungry people away from here.
Give them to eat, lest on their way they faint."
The disciples, perplexed, said with complaint:

"We have not enough for this multitude to eat.
Not all the lunches around would the task complete."
"Use what you have," the wondrous master said.
They replied, "Two small fishes and five loaves of bread."

The lad who gave Jesus his lunch watched amazed,
While Jesus blessed and broke the bread, into heaven gazed.
Multiplied the small lunch for all to eat.
Humbly they all watched with wonder at His feet.

He supplied the need, but He wasn't through.
Jesus gave command to gather the fragments, too.
Twelve baskets were gathered at the end of the meal.
All were satisfied; each one had their fill.

When things are rough and we're up against the wall,
We know to look to Jesus lest we fall.
He cares and will never forsake His child.
He's always there, regardless how much we're reviled.

If we ask in His name, believing His word,
We can rest assured our prayers will be heard.
The Bible says He can do beyond what we comprehend;

He wants to fill not only the need, but the baskets send
To show His mighty power so the fragments will be
A reminder of the overwhelming love for you and me.

# GOD'S WAITING ROOM

When we have been made to wait for
what we want in life, we are pressed.
We feel unexplainable pauses are worthless:
we become distressed.
It's God putting us in His waiting room,
creating a new masterpiece.
We complain, neglecting to hear His voice,
longing for a release.
When we should be quietly resting
in His promises, trusting His grace,
His mighty handiwork in progress while we linger,
seeking His face.

As we look in the Bible,
Abraham decided to hurry God's promise along.
But it wasn't God's plan; because Abraham
didn't wait, things went wrong.
Chaos continued with his offspring
and the family had to part.
All because Abraham wasn't willing
to be patient and follow God's heart,
Unfortunately altered the way in
which the Lord's plan was fulfilled.
God's timing was not understood,
so it was difficult for Abraham to yield.

In this waiting room, we find the
fruit of His vineyards and bountiful blessings.
Preparing us for ministry and receiving instruction,
it's a room for dressing.
Or maybe it's a place to hide away
from ill surroundings or wrangling.

# THE MASTER'S TOUCH

A needed quiet time of purifying and
correction from the worldly entangling.
Lord, renew in us the strength
as the eagle, while we wait on You.
Let integrity and righteousness
be our character as we ensue,

Strengthen us as we wait in this secret place,
expecting the promises You declared,
A precious time of abiding and communion
we so seldom have shared.
Resting in Your love with tranquility and patience,
Continuing in Your work, enduring without complacence.
Let us abide in the same calling wherein You have appointed,
Being instant in season and out,
steadfast in that You've anointed.

# HE'LL BE A FRIEND

My eyes may be blinded, the road I cannot see,
But I'm assured my God knows what's best for me.
Sometimes I don't understand what He has planned.
One thing I can do is hold to His mighty hand.

He's touched by my feelings; He understands the pain.
Step into His presence and be renewed again.
Come into the Shakina glory, that balm in Gilead,
Give the problem to Jesus, the best friend one has ever had.

He's a friend whose love knows no limit: He'll never let you down.
He is the mighty defender and has power that abounds.
His arm is there to lift you, guide you, and see you through.
He'll be your strength in the weak times: He'll be a friend to you.

He will be a friend and guide.
Give you power inside.
His love has no limit.
He's that kind of friend.

# I AM HE

Wounded, hurting heart, grieving over a lost loved one,
There is One who stands by you, waiting
To be a true friend and comfort so near
Whispering, I am He.

Pain wracks your body hours without end,
Nothing seems to give the relief needed to rest.
There is one whose stripes were given to heal.
Saying, I am He.

Problems come your way and seem so great.
Just how can you see your way clear,
Longing for an advocate to take your case?
There is One takes your every burden,
Stating, I am He.

Guilt weighs us down; anger eats at our very soul.
Love, happiness, and hope seem so very far away.
But salvation is as near as the name of Jesus.
Just say Jesus and He will answer,
I AM HE.

# I'M FREE

The chains that bound me had slowed me to a crawl.
Then finally I could not function; no, not at all.
Desperately one day I fell to a place of prayer.
But there was nothing, I didn't feel God there.

Hours passed by and I pleaded and paced the floor,
But all I did or said was only beat on heaven's door.
Words flowed from my lips but not a tear could fall.
I tried to repent and on the name of Jesus call.

Drunken with weariness, pain, and long-wanted sleep,
I was determined to feel God's presence sweep.
Kneeling, standing still, or pacing the floor,
I tried everything I knew to open heaven's door.

Exasperated, desperate, and helpless I fell across my bed.
Exhausted physically, delirious from the pounding in my head.
"Lord, here I am. Do heart surgery like only You can do.
I cannot carry on like this, so it's up to You."

Finally admitting my sin broke each chain that had me bound.
Tears of repentance came, so did His presence surround.
God did surgery, breaking the chains that held me fast.
But praise God, only Jesus did it. I'm free at last.

# I'M TIRED: I'M READY FOR MY MIRACLE.

Pride becomes baggage as we travel this terrain.
The baggage gets heavier as we each success gain.
We become proud of all the things that we have done,
With the accomplishments and trophies that we have won.
We try to keep up with things we are expected to do,
Having a facade - not letting our real personality come through.
I'm tired:  I could use a miracle.

Our relationships become difficult;
it's another baggage we tolerate.
It's not our fault and often unforgiveness turns to hate.
The load is getting heavier, but we carry it nonetheless.
We get used to the burden, refusing our sins to confess.
We keep to ourselves, thinking everyone else is immoral.
So often we are the reason for many a quarrel.
I'm tired and need a miracle.

We run in directions that God hasn't chosen for us to trod,
And wonder why we are not well enough to serve God.
Our bodies are in poor health, in urgent need of mending.
He wants us to slow down; we need to start surrendering.
We miss many promises God wants for us in this life,
Because we are caught up with all its busyness and strife.
I'm tired and desire a miracle.

We go through life pretending to have the victory,
But deep down in our hearts hidden is great misery.
We live with the baggage of secret sins,
Not letting anyone close know what is within.
We try to live the Christian life without God's Spirit
Hoping that no one will ever know, secretly fear it.
I'm tired: I've got to have a miracle.

THE MASTER'S TOUCH

All our baggage becomes too heavy,
 and we become constrained,
When we could be delivered, and victory could be obtained.
Jesus said, "Come all ye who are heavy laden,
and I will give you rest."
He wants to take all your worries and give you His best.
We just need to come to the Master for a cleansing rain,
Leave all our baggage at the cross with all the pain.
I tired: I'm ready for my miracle.

# IF I CAN DO THIS THING WILLINGLY

The task, no matter how big or small,
I find myself examining one and all
Who could be a better candidate for the task.
So, I often hesitate to do what I'm asked.
Oh! That I should realize what God wants of me,
And whatever is for my brother will be.
Lord, help me to accept the task for me
Only if I can do this thing willingly.

There are times I wonder if the Lord knows best,
When I'm faced with an insurmountable test.
How can I give Him glory and praise
When I can't seem to understand His ways.
Thinking on whatsoever is good, lovely, and pure,
I have this assurance in Him I'm secure.
Knowing that whatever comes, it's His will for me.
So now I can do this thing willingly.

If we could learn that it's fasting and prayer
Casting those weights that beset us into His care.
Letting God increase so the world can only see,
Yielding servants, we on this earth can be.
Learning to accept the path as His direction.
Accepting each test as a tool of perfection.
Then I know that I can do whatever I'm asked
Yes, I can do this thing willingly.

# LEAN ON ME

Dear Lord, I feel I've gone to my journey's end.
On this earth, I have not one friend.
My burden is more than I can bear.
Of trouble and heartaches, I've had my share.

The road is lonely, and oh so bleak,
All is darkness, step by step I seek.
I've walked in Your statutes best I know how,
And which way to turn, I know not now.

A burdened heart and a mind that's shattered,
Only serving You, Lord, is what really matters.
Give me new strength to carry my burden,
Or faith to surrender them, so I'll be certain.

I listened as I finished my prayer,
A gentle voice and a calmness were there.
He touched me and gave an inner glow,
A greater peace only He could bestow.

"I've gone through it too, my dear little one.
I carried My cross and for yours have come.
So lean on Me, my little sheep,
Leave your burden with Me to keep.

"I'm right by your side and companion will be.
I'm your problem solver if you'll leave it to Me.
Lean on Me, my child, lean on Me.
Give Me your every burden, lean on Me."

# ORDINARY PEOPLE
# WITH GOD'S POWER

There are times we are afraid during many days of our life.
We coward back, finding ourselves bowed down with strife.
A feeling of failure grips our hearts, and we tend not to try.
What's the use, we will be a disappointment again, is our sigh.
But as God's children we often fail to understand
God has given us the strength to do whatever is in His plan.

Elisha was just an ordinary man that listened to God's voice.
It was up to him to hear God and make the right choice.
As the King of Syria threatened
God's people with secret attacks,
Elisha had the courage to let Israel's king in on all the facts.
It messed up the enemy's plan and
made the Syrian army understand.
God has His children protected and
safe in the palm of His hand.

As a believer, we have the power every situation to overcome.
Greater is He that is in you than Satan's enticing to succumb.
God has promised to work exceeding greatness in our favor,
According to the effectual power of our wonderful Savior.
God has not given us the spirit of fear, but love and sound mind.
Complete in Him, who conquers all principalities we'll find.

He can do exceedingly abundantly above all that we think or ask.
He is willing and capable to give power to do whatever the task.
We are kept by His power through our faith,
for temptations we face
Which will keep us until He says,
"Well done, you've finished the race!"
We, that dwell in Him and He in us,
will have the power for every trial,
Knowing the crown of life is waiting for His children all the while.

# ROLL AWAY THE STONE

Jesus stood at the tomb of Lazarus and wept
with sorrowful tears.
Family and friends gathered with Him,
a friend He had known for years.
He said, as all the group was wondering what
He would do next,
He commands the stone to be rolled away -
not what the crowd expects.

There were a few that made their apprehensions
known to the Master.
Opening the tomb, they explained,
would give a stink that would be a disaster.
But Jesus could not do what He came to
do with the stone in its place.
He needed it moved away so He
could work His miracle and grace.

Once the tomb was opened and
He was given access to the demise
He used His power to bring forth
His dead friend and dry teary eyes.
Had the stone not been rolled
away for the Master's divine touch
The dead friend would have stayed
in the tomb, not worth much.

Jesus is still giving the word to give Him
access to things we have buried,
That have become lost and dead,
burdensome, ever to be carried.
We bury broken relationship and
hidden anger mounting deep inside,

Hoping no one will know the
unforgiveness we are trying to hide.
Keeping all the wrong all bottled up
in the crevasses of our soul,
The stench of the dead and rotten
things smells beyond our control.
We try to keep the stone on the tomb
of all the things we long to reveal,
Due to the heaviness and the smell
that we battle to conceal.

For some it is dreams that seem
like will never come to fruition.
Time is slipping away, hopes of that long aspiration
gone from one's vision.
Always remembering if I could only
have a little more time or money.
Never had a chance, seeing it for others just not funny.

God wants us to open those fractured
and broken places that give you pain,
But He can only do what is best for us as
we allow Him access to gain.
We are the only ones that roll the stone
away and reveal the wounded spaces.
He wants and will put healing salve
on the stinking and hurting places.

He commands us to roll the stone away,
so He can clean all the putrid stenches.
No longer as a "walking sepulcher,"
but a revived vessel from Satan's clenches.
God will be a deliverer, healer, peacemaker
and restore one with His Spirit.
Allow us to walk in the newness of
life facing life without fearing it.

# STILL IN HIS HANDS

With all the struggles I faced, my life was spinning around.
I couldn't understand why all the ups and downs.
When I finally turned to the Master He said, "It was His will."
He had picked me up and placed me on His potter's wheel.

Indeed, the Potter had put me on His spinning wheel,
Washing and forming me for His purpose to fulfill
His skillful hands molded this vessel with great design.
Preparing this piece of clay for a plan divine.

The good times were the blessings He splashed on this clay,
Giving me encouragement to continue in His way.
He let me know that it wasn't what He saw right then,
But what He saw could be when He was finished within.

When I thought He had completed the task on the wheel
He crumbled my world and many questions in my mind filled.
"Your vessel was marred, and it couldn't be used in that class.
There was a blemish in your vessel and it would never last."

The problem wasn't with the potter or His spinning wheel,
It was in this lump of clay – the hardness He could feel.
So, the Potter remakes by the touch of His merciful hand
To repair the marred vessel to fit in His perfect plan.

We don't always understand every one of life's stages,
But we do have One we can rely on when everything rages,
Through the many failures all we need to do is stand.
For whatever may be the crises, we're still in His hands.

# THE EYE OF THE STORM

As I started out on my way,
The sun shone bright as day
No mountain or hill too steep to climb.
God is with me, so things would be fine.
My goal in plain view
I was confident in what I was to do.

Then the clouds hung low
The wind came and the rain was cold.
I found myself in the midst of the storm.
My soul became weary,
My feet slipping, I was so tired,
Longing for the eye of the storm.

The storm I'm in may be
What He wants for me.
But my response, my purpose
Is what determines my destiny.
I can't give up or let fear be my guide.
I'm trusting in God
Because He's always by my side.

If the clouds must hang low
The wind comes and the rain is cold,
And I find myself amid the storm,
My soul may be weary,
My feet may slip, I may be tired,
But God has for me an eye of the storm.

# THE KING NEVER SLEEPS

King Ahasuerus couldn't sleep, neither
letting his servants see rest.
"Bring the book of records of the chronicles"
was his royal request.
In the recitation, it was made known
Mordecai's loyalty to the King.
The King was overcome with gratitude,
wondered the kind of honoring.

He was concerned when he heard no reward was provided.
As a result, he inquired of his court
of what reward should be decided.
Haman in the outer court ready
for the honor the king should render.
Thinking for himself, gave a pomp
rendition of honor and splendor.

It pleased the king and commanded
Haman to carry out the event.
Haman was angry, carried out the king's delight,
plotted without relent.
Despite whatever he plotted it seemed everything to be foiled
But he tried all the harder, greater, and worse things he toiled.

We have a king that never sleeps, never slumbers even at night,
Who is delighted in blessing us even when things aren't right.
It doesn't matter what trouble or problems we go through,
Or what our enemies may seem to plot or plan to do.

It's because we have a Heavenly Father always giving direction,
Conquering our enemies, preventing their deception.
The battle may seem unbearable and our life cumbers.
But we have a King that never sleeps nor slumbers.

# THE SCOURGING PLACE

Praying in the garden of Gethsemane,
Jesus, facing the greatest trial,
Struggling to take the easy way out, knowing the last mile.
He fell on His face, pleading for the cup to pass,
His heart crushed with grief.
With the weight of sin of the world on His shoulders,
He found no relief.

It was an assignment that He had to go through, He resigned,
Putting His heart and will in His Father's hand as assigned.
Not His will to go through the scourging, ridicule, and pain,
He had to go through this before the power and authority to gain.

In the garden is where He prepared
His heart for the hours ahead,
Knowing He had committed His life
and spirit in His Father's will to be led.
His disciples didn't really understand
the depth of what lay in store.
As time went on, Jesus realized this
assignment lurking at the door.

The night was long, as high priest and
elders led him from place to place,
Making accusations before the courts,
trying to find someone to agree with the disgrace.
Striking Him, beating, thinking this would
make Him change His mind and retract,
Pressing a crown of thorns on His head,
putting a robe on open wounds on His back.

A night of mocking and scorn continued beating amid the throng.
Jeering, if He was king of the Jews, save Himself,
each finding something wrong.
Yet He never opened His mouth in all the turmoil,
this spotless Lamb.
He knew who He was, and it gave Him the confidence to stand.

It seemed He was losing and all He had taught
succumbed to a tragic culmination.
Those that followed were scattered and this kingdom
He spoke of, in defamation.
It was all in God's plan to redeem mankind,
that they would receive adoption,
To become sons and be free from iniquity
and cleansed from corruption.

Jesus was our example, to go through those
tests that we would rather avoid,
Thinking this affliction process is a crushing
feeling as if we are being destroyed.
It is the trial of one's faith, tried by fire,
brings praise, honor and glory – the Lord's plan.
Jesus, being the author and finisher of our faith,
now sitting on God's right hand.

We have a high priest that is touched
with the feeling of our infirmities,
And acquainted with grief, experienced hate,
bruised for our iniquities.
At the end of the test,
we know the greatness and power of the God we serve.
We learn the goodness and patience that
is given and so undeserved.

What we lose in the fight seems like a great loss,
but God uses what is left for His glory.
Those who leave and don't understand the full
meaning of our conflict or story.
Some will stand afar off watching what you will do or how you
in the end will fare.
Few will pray for you or go through the battle, whatever way
they can and be there.

As Jesus prepared His heart so must we be equipped for what-
ever our assignment,
Having the right attitude to withstand the duration of the test,
our heart in alignment.
He that endures shall be saved and will receive the crown of
everlasting life,
Overcoming the enemy and his wiles, persistent in the Word
during all his strife.

The cross experience during the test will bring the right under-
standing in power.
Those who are faithful enduring temptation receive the crown
in God's appointed hour.
God will honor your love for righteousness and anoint you with
the oil of pleasure,
Rewarding your faith and consistancy in His kingdom and
authority beyond measure.

# TOO BUSY

Life gets so hurried we wonder what to do first.
We miss those dear ones who cry, I hunger and thirst.
I've not heard that lately in this land of plenty.
It's only because we're "so busy" we're empty,
Void and insensitive to man or God's command,
The list of our wants is first in demand.

The dear brother has a burden: please just a minute of time.
Take a number, I'm busy right now, wait in line.
The schedule gets tough, not knowing which way to turn,
It'll be great when people God's way will learn.
My body gets numb and wishes for a pillow for my head.
Oh, why can't there be a rest as the Word has said.

A man cries out with behavior we feel uncouth.
But we can't read between the lines, "I need the truth."
Anger rises, we despise such a creature that has no care,
When it's such a soul crying out, "I want you to share,
What a child of God has captured within one's heart."
Walking hurriedly by "too busy," to do one's part.

A simple hello or a kind gesture is done.
A touch, a handshake from everyone.
Not a soul knows a need even exists.
"God bless you," we find ourselves in a hurried run.
To understand because of the web we've spun.

We so often are caught up in how we appear
In the sight of man that God can't be near.
Our social surroundings confine our view,
That man's cries can't come through.
How swiftly we learn to overwork instead of overflow.
The wisdom of living is a life of overflowing,
Not mistaking his will for a life of going.

# WHEN GUILT TURNS TO GRATITUDE

Everyone in the house was watching
with bantering words to their peers.
Why was this woman kneeling at Jesus feet,
washing His feet with Her tears?
No one understood her actions as she
worshipped in a way that made them gasp.
Only she knew what Jesus had done,
delivering her from so much guilt of her past.

It occurs even today as those that carry
their guilt and pain not knowing what to do.
Trudging through their life hiding behind a
smile, rest, or peace they have not a clue.
Our healing comes when we drop our
arrogance and selfish pride,
Throwing ourselves on the mercy of God,
repenting, everything in Him confide.

We gather and have church, a service,
and a time of singing with saints as a norm,
And often we make excuses for missing
even if it becomes a form.
We've not experienced the freeing power
that God wants us to attain.
He wants us to stop the excuses, repent and find freedom in
Him, to obtain.

A true repentance, a "don't care what people think"
worship only comes when
We surrender our guilt and shame, completely admit all our sin.
True praise only comes when the weight
of the burden of guilt is gone.
Guilt that brings repentance is a powerful change
and an overflowing song.

We are thankful. We count our blessings
of what the Lord has performed.
He is the lifter of the head and guilt releaser,
a deliverer from the storm.
Our hearts are thankful for that power and
anointing that fixes the wrong,
No more guilt but gratitude giving a new
level in God's kingdom strong.

There is a guilt that we can't change,
a loss of a child or a marriage that we can't fix.
We can say we are sorry, but the words have stung,
a relationship with conflicts.
How do I fix it, it doesn't seem to get better,
I wished it would go away.
I could say I'm sorry, but healing will
take time no matter what I try to say.

It's when we have fallen on our knees,
what can make me whole again?
There's no other fount I know, precious
is the flow; I need to rid the pain.
Nothing but the blood of Jesus.
No one else can fix and take the guilt away.
But the Lord is standing and waiting,
and so gently hear Him say,

I was wounded for your transgression,
punished for your shame, bruised for your iniquity,
I bore the rebuke for your peace and
provided healing in the stripe's indignity.
I have already paid the bill; there is no need
to carry such a heavy and unnecessary weight.
I am offering a garment of praise for the spirit
of heaviness; it's for all, please don't wait.

In My kingdom, there is no condemnation;
who I set free is free indeed.
There is a place for all that will come;
the invitation stands for all greed.
Cast your cares on Me, for no other
can take the hidden pain and grief.
I have come to give life and for your
guilt offer victorious relief.

No one else can give God praise
for the blessing you have received,
For all those hidden pains that no
one else could ever perceive.
You are the one that can praise God
for struggles you've overcome,
With gratitude for His mercy, forgiveness,
and for the battles He has won.

# WORTH THE STRUGGLE

The Lord told Rebecca there were two
nations to which she was to give birth.
There would be two manner of people
 that would rule on the earth.
One people would be stronger,
but the elder was to serve the young.
The first was called Esau and Jacob
followed; to his brother's heel he clung.

Jacob was making pottage, tempting
Esau's appetite, famished, and frayed.
Feed me, Esau command, some of your
pottage, an opportunity conveyed.
Swearing that day, the birthright was
Jacob's rightful blessing, however shrewd.
Esau's appetite satisfied, went his way
despising what he should have valued.

The struggle bred between brothers
as they grew each with different personalities.
Mom catered to the younger and Dad to the older,
adding to unchecked anxieties.
As their father lay ready to give his last breath,
a race for the honor and blessing bent.
Rebecca abetted Jacob in deceiving his father
to honor him with the birthright endowment.

One may wonder if there was really
supposed to be a struggle all of Jacob's life.
God had said He would honor and bless him,
but there was that constant strife.
Leaving home, headed for a land he had
never seen before, discord and subjugation.

What was his life going to be like;
was this birthright worth the rejection?

Sometimes we need to stand up
for what is rightfully ours.
We don't understand the road we
have to travel or heartache for hours.
Following a road and seeking the
right place to obtain God's approval,
Finding that God-encounter,
experiencing peace and anguish removal.

Jacob traveled to a place where he found
blessings in the face of deceit.
He was in the place God wanted him to be,
overcoming defeat.
Blessed with wives, children, and cattle,
doing whatever his hands found to do,
Seeing how God worked on his behalf
year after year, blessings ensue.

As Jacob experienced the struggle
with the angel all alone in the night
He was determined to make once and
for all the end of the approval plight.
The angel wanted to leave at the break of day,
after a long contesting.
Jacob didn't give in without a blessing,
knowing whom he was wrestling.

The angel blessed him with a new name
that would give him a fresh start,
A new way of walking and peace knowing
the acceptance of God in his heart.
His thigh was touched and he limped for
the rest of his years.

But there he found God's approval and
release of apprehension and fears.

One may labor for position, wealth, and honor,
every step perplexing,
When we really need to know who we are in God,
in His favor resting,
Knowing what God wants in our lives
when things seem to be so wrong.
The favor is yours when you find the
place where God says you belong.

Stand on God's promises, trust in the
Word He has put in your heart.
Wait for His timing and make sure
His will is done from the start.
The battle is not yours; God is on your side.
Keep the assurance
When you have God's favor,
victory is coming with great endurance.

# CHILDREN ARE OUR HERITAGE

# A HEART OF A CHILD

The disciples discussed who was greatest in their midst.
Jesus answered their question, "Simply it's this,
Humbling yourself to God as one of these"
As He beckoned a little child to His knees.

He who serves will be the greatest among men.
A willing heart and life available are when
God can use a soul who learns self-denial.
Coming to Him unreserved with the heart of a child.

Doing a simple task with faith that can't be measured,
Yielding in His presence with a heart so treasured.
Having a life that's pliable and so easily styled
By God, so He can give us a heart of a child.

# GOD'S GIFT

We were elated when God said you would arrive.
It was with great delight, so hard to describe.
Our hearts filled with wonder to look into your face.
You are God's to gift to us, your tiny life to embrace.

We were chosen, your precious life to teach and mold,
And count it a great responsibility and honor to hold.
So we will love you and do the very best we can
To guide and instruct you by example in God's plan,

We may not be perfect, but we know God will get us through.
A Godly life is what we want to try to model for you.
Despite our shortcomings and the mistakes along the way
To observe your love for God would be no greater day.

Serving Christ will be your gift to us, our dream fulfilled,
To observe you, give your life, to God completely yield.
Whatever accomplishments your life may lead,
You can find in Christ whatever you need.


In honor of our grandson

# OUR ANGEL'S WINGS

Every good and perfect gift comes from God, it's true.
We can see that when we look at you.
We pray God gives you wings of gladness, bringing delight,
The kind of joy that will sustain you both day and night.

Richness of His presence to be your constant guide,
Abiding in the secret place, you learn to hide.
May He give wings of protection from each trial,
Walking safely with your hand in His all the while.

In everything your hand finds to do,
May the favor of God rest upon you.
Your wings of blessings will follow you each step of the way,
As you walk in His will each and every day.

Nothing shall offend those that love God's Word and His voice,
As you seek His face and make Him your choice.
We ask God for wings of contentment as you run this race.
May the glory of the Lord shine continually on your face.


In honor of our granddaughter

# OUR PRINCESS

Early in the morning we anxiously awaited your delivery date.
It was exciting when God said we no longer needed to wait.
We know you have a place in this family no matter the size.
We're glad to make room for each offspring and its cries.

You have a sibling that adores you beyond what words can reveal.
We watched how each event has shown love's appeal.
Each time those expressions are so lovingly rendered,
Sometimes awkwardly, and those so fittingly tendered.

We're preparing you for your purpose that God has planned,
Equipping you for His service and placing you in His hand.
We are only guardians, and strive to be examples for you to see,
But it will be up to you to accomplish all God wants you to be.

We understand the privilege of having you in our care is a pleasure,
So circumspectly and respectfully, we live before you in measure.
You are a gift that has been placed here by our heavenly King,
A princess was given to us,
so we our adoration and gratitude bring.


In honor of our granddaughter

# THERE'S A JOY IN TEACHING

There's a joy in teaching, and I found it to be true.
The more you talk about Jesus, the more real He is to you.
You talk until you can't say any more,
More than you ever thought!
Just keep on teaching about my Lord;
Salvation has been brought.

Yes, there's a joy in teaching, and I found it to be true.
The more you do for Jesus, there's always more to do.
It's not only on Sunday morning
That you need to be in tune,
But daily reading your Bible
And often with Him commune.

Oh! There's a joy in teaching and I found it to be so.
You get into your lesson and find you're stepping on toes,
There's is no turning aside, when it's right.
Give me the words to say
So they'll see the light.

Whew! There's a joy in teaching, I know it to be true.
The louder you talk about Jesus, the louder they chatter, too.
Yes, you're trying to do what you feel best,
And you wonder what went wrong.
Dear Jesus, help me,
Dear Lord, my patience won't last long.

Yes, there's a joy in teaching and I found it to be true.
I love to talk about Jesus and everything he can do.
Yes, I love my Primary class,
Their ages, seven and eight.
For wisdom and grace, dear Lord,
To guide their footsteps straight.

# WHAT'S IN YOUR CHILD'S LUNCHBOX?

Throughout the years we make lunches and go on our merry way.
Sometimes the meal is tasty or maybe
not so interesting for the day.
Some think of what's best tasting or the calorie intake
Or use intriguing ideas with food so the meal will be ate.

We have the privilege to contribute to our children's wellbeing.
Their physical, mental, and spiritual
health should be our overseeing.
We call the doctor when they have an illness or a cold.
There to give a hug, listen to them or be there each to hold.

It seems the spiritual health of our children lacks some thought.
We are so busy and really don't have time;
God's Word is not taught.
This is when we should live out and
implement lessons in different ways,
Creating things that the kids can think
about throughout their days.

Put in the "Bread" of Life and a note
will remind them of Jesus' style.
Maybe remind them on the fruit cup a
fruit of the Spirit applying with a smile.
A bag of chips, God can take the pieces
when something goes wrong,
Using all the brokenness of a puzzle
trying to make us strong.

Put an apple in; so many to choose,
whether red, yellow, or green,
Whatever color we like, just remember
with God's eye we are seen.

Add a paper heart with words;
God is looking for a humble heart to please.
Pure, clean, and honest wherever we find God our path leads.

A Bible lesson like the lad's lunch of five loaves and two fish,
Can be reminded when a tuna sandwich is the main dish.
The item that doesn't seem to be the favorite can be understood,
Reminding one some things coming
one's way can be for our good.

Give them their spiritual food in their lunch a little at a time.
This will help them grow as you add a simple note or line.
It will keep their mind on what God wants them to do.
So, He can help them grow with the little note from you.

# GETTING MY
# PRAISE ON!

# ALABASTER OF PRAISE

Everyone in the house knew what Mary had brought.
They could see the alabaster box, and how she sought
To kneel before Jesus and use her long hair,
Washing His feet with her tears as if no one was there.

The odor of the costly perfume filled all the room,
But the purpose of her heart was consumed.
Realizing what the Master in her life had done,
It didn't matter what was said by anyone.

Forgiveness for a life of sin and shame,
A new life was hers because Jesus came.
Gratitude from her heart overflowed in such a way,
It didn't matter what anyone around her had to say.

So we find it still in this day and time;
Those that have been delivered are also inclined
To give their worship with utmost of praise
Often meeting with the scoffer's gaze.

It's only those that have been through the costly trial
That will find that it's not hard for self-denial.
This kind of praise comes with a great price,
Treasured far more than when nothing is sacrificed.

# BLESSINGS OVERFLOWING

Observe to keep God's commandments and walk in His way.
Be strong and of good courage with life's challenges today.
Speak of His goodness from early morning until late at night;
Continually honor the Lord with all your heart, soul and might.

Then shall you prosper beyond your fondest passion,
Overtaken with God's blessings in His majestic fashion.
He has set His love on you, guiding
you through many rough roads.
He has chosen you, redeemed you,
the lifter of life's loads.

He has established you just for Himself,
the greatest of foundations,
Strong enough to endure from generations to generations.
Making you the head, and not the tail,
with promotions fitly assigned
Opening His good treasures with rain
in its season, providentially designed.

Everyone will know you and call you by His name.
God will promote you as His greatness you proclaim.
You will not be afraid of the enemies at your door:
For God will scatter them many ways the more.

Your fields and gardens will overflow,
your table abundant with radiant hue.
He will plague your enemies with diseases
that were planned for you.
Wherever you place your feet shall be yours to possess.
Counsel will sit at your feet your wisdom to address.

The crown of your heart shall be the fruit of your womb.
Joy and peace shall be in your house, each and every room.
All these blessings are yours as God's commandments you obey.
So, start your day with His statutes in your heart:
Be well on your way.

# BOUNTIFUL BLESSINGS

A heart full of thanksgiving I offer to You, O Lord,
For Your bountiful blessings that only Your love can afford.
I love You because You have heard my supplications.
Surely Your mercy endures to all generations.

Your words are a lamp unto my feet, a light unto my pathway.
You tenderly guide me at the dawning of each new day.
You hide me in your secret pavilion in a time of need.
My strong deliverer, through each battle, my captain, you lead.

Far exceeds any blessing is Your eternal peace.
Where there'll be no more sorrow, all strife will cease.
I thank You, Lord, for the opportunity of serving You humbly,
Awaiting the day, we can spend together eternally.

Our praises will flow through the ages, the Hallelujahs ring.
When we've crossed the shores of heaven to meet Jesus, our King.
Time will be no more; our bodies won't need to rest.
We can sing of how we got over and we're truly blessed.

# GOD'S CREATION

The rushing waters sing a song of God's power.
The thunder announces adoration of His majesty.
The gangly cedars bow down their lofty tower.
The ocean's perpetual wave resounds His boundless mercy.

The diamonds resonate with a sparkle of His countenance.
The rocks render the cleft of His steadfast security.
The olive drops oil of His merciful deliverance.
The flames fashion the magnificence of His purity.

All His creation is given to display affirmation,
For man to offer God his greatest delight.
The perfect design of His creation
To serve and praise God with all its might.

# MAKE ME TO HEAR YOUR GLADNESS

Though I walk in the midst of trouble
Darkness on every side
It's only by His mercy when we stumble,
In His strength we abide

When I'm overwhelmed, He's my refuge,
Shelter from the storm
My deliverer from sin's prison
His wonders to perform.

We shall do valiantly through every test
When we hold our peace and let God do the rest
Stand on His promises, trust Him one step at a time.
Praise Him through your trial and you will find.

Lord, make me to hear Your gladness.
Restore unto me Your joy.
Let my tongue sing Your praises.
Let me stand before You broken
In Your presence with a sacrifice of praise.
Lord, make to hear Your gladness
The rest of my days.

# REJOICE

My brethren, rejoice when you go through
different tests along the way.
Just know that the confidence you
place in God will be your stay.
This testing produces patience of your faith,
so let it have its perfect control,
That you may be flawless and complete,
lacking naught in your soul.

If you lack wisdom, ask of God,
who bountifully gives to those that ask.
Without finding fault or reproach
will give to him for every difficult task.
Put your confidence in God without doubting,
the Word does commend.
For he who doubts is like a wave of the sea
driven and tossed by the wind.

Let not a man suppose without faith
receive anything that intercedes
Because he is a double-minded man,
unsteady in all his deeds.
Let the lowly glory in the Lord whom
exalts as we make Him our roots
And the rich walk in humiliation,
considering riches fade away in his pursuits.

Blessed is the man who endures temptation;
for when he has overcome,
Will receive the crown of life because
faith puts the devil on the run.
This is a promise to those who love God, submitted to His will.
Sufficient strength and courage in each of His children to fill.

Do not be misled, my beloved brethren;
every good gift is from above.
Trust in His Word, in God there is no
discrepancy or change in His love.
Lay aside all uncleanness and receive with
meekness the grafted word,
Which is able to save your souls because
of the commands you've heard.

Tribulations bring forth patience;
this in turn gives our hearts confidence.
In His power and birthed in us the
Word showing us His evidence
Be swift to hear, slow to speak,
casting away any haughtiness.
Put off all anger, ill intentions, filthy
communication, or naughtiness.

Jesus was tempted in all points as we;
the lust of the fleshly desires,
The pride of life and the temptations
our eyes often conspires.
But we have a high priest that is touched
with our feelings in our soul,
Bidding us to come to His throne humbly,
assured of His control.

We are more than conquers through Him who loves us indeed,
Who is able and willing to give us grace and mercy in time of need.
Now God is faithful making a way our temptation to overcome.
It's our privilege being His child to attain power of His Kingdom.

# TIME TO CELEBRATE

This a time of praise and worship to
God that has brought us until today.
The road has not been easy, but His
power and love has made a way.
We celebrate His faithfulness,
which is given every morning new,
Resting on His promises through
the years carrying us through.

We celebrate the song that He put in the heart,
a weapon against the storm.
The music in the heart that has made our
character, molding to His form,
Singing a song the angels may never sing or understand,
But we worship our Lord for His strength and mighty hand.

We celebrate the Word which we hide in our hearts and mind,
Quoting it over and over until
we get the answer we need to find.
We celebrate the rock that we know
will be there when all else fails,
Leaning on what God has said in all the wiles and gales.

A celebration of a soul giving their
life to serve our wonderful Lord,
Receiving the precious Holy Spirit,
finding mercy in one accord,
The angels celebrate the soul coming to
love our great King.
This is a celebration that makes the
whole heaven's inhabitants sing.

What a celebration, as the people
come together in harmony
Working for one good, God's kingdom, soldiers in God's army,
A purpose that is not our own, but harvesting the lost
Withstanding the tempest, whatever it may cost.

# WHEN I'VE COUNTED ALL MY BLESSINGS THEN I CAN COMPLAIN

Often, I can see the bad in a situation.
It's no good, is the conclusion of my evaluation.
Then the Lord reminds me to begin to attain
By counting all my blessings before I complain.

There is a roof over my head, a warm place to sleep,
Food on the table, and even if dirty, clothes by the heap.
And too, there's my job to help my personal gain.
Remember, I'm counting my blessings before I complain.

The Lord's been my provider, protector, and friend.
There's His mercy, and what a guide He's been.
He lights the earth with sunshine and waters it with rain.
When I've counted all my blessings, then I can complain.

He takes a life, shattered and broken, and makes it brand new.
He answers my prayers, keeps His promises, and follows through.
He's never let me down, my steps He's ordained;
With all these blessings, who has time to complain!

# PRAYER CHANGES
# EVERYTHING

# A CLEAN HEART

I asked the Lord for a clean heart while down on my knees.
Take everything that shouldn't be there; do as You please.
Indeed, He did as I asked of Him and so much more.
He does His good pleasure if we'll open our heart's door.

He looked around, then threw out fear and doubt.
"These can't stay here," He said. "They've got to be thrown out."
He threw out things I thought really could remain,
But He said that later they would cause great pain.

Next were my thoughts, some good and some bad.
He checked very carefully; I noticed the concern he had.
"These are not pure, nor lovely, nor have any virtue at all.
Keeping these thoughts will cause you to fall."

My secrets are the hardest to keep like I should.
Explaining, I reminded Him I did the best I could.
But He opened every secret, big and small.
He took them out until He had them all.

He spent time so sweetly to dine and sup.
Remember this is My blood, drink from this cup.
Take this bread and in doing so remember Me.
Here's My Word; read it and fruitful be.

Then took His cleansing power and scrubbed the place well,
Turned and said, "It must stay like this for Me to dwell.
I give you power to walk in a clean, holy way.
But you must keep your heart clean each and every day."

# FRUITFUL MINISTRY

Hannah longed to be fruitful like Peninnah, Elkanah's other wife.
But as time went on, she was barren,
only bringing heartache and strife.
Elkanah loved both wives and showered
Hannah with love so great,
But Peninnah's provoking brought Hannah's longing heart hate.

This desperation in the depths of
her soul plagued her day after day,
Sending Hannah to her knees in tears and agony to pray.
She wouldn't eat or drink in bitterness until this thing was done,
Asking God to smile on her and give her a dear little son.

We, as Christians, find ourselves unfruitful
in ministry of the Lord,
Feeling unloved and left out while others
are praised and adored,
When God is taking us through His
time of shaping and molding
So, the ministry we are to do will glorify him as it's unfolding.

So, let the Peninnahs in your life provoke you to passion.
To be a fruitful bough, birthing in
you only what God can fashion.
When God brings forth the fruit as
we yield to His will and are anointed,
It's then we can know and bring forth
the work as He has appointed.

Just remember, we're not what we will be until God is finished.
We may have to be put in the fire, purged, our will diminished.
We've gone from Egypt, through
the wilderness, and now in Jordan's river,
But when we enter Canaan's land, God will a fruitful work deliver.

# HANNAH IS COMING

Hannah entered the church with bitterness of soul.
Her load was so great, her heart she tried to unfold.
The minister saw how burdened she was without sound.
He mistook her sorrow for going beyond her bounds.

Baring her soul before the Lord with her petition,
With a heavy heart and extreme contrition
She cried earnestly unto God for her heart's desire,
So great it was, as passionate as fire.

Oh, for a child that would be all her own.
She would give him back before he was grown.
The minister gave her an expression; her prayer was heard.
She arose and quietly took him at his word.

In time she brought the son to the church to live,
She knelt down and to God glory and honor give.
Worship was joyful and exalted her Lord of salvation,
A heart of gladness and extreme adulation

Still today we have Hannah coming to pray
With great compassionate burden in her way
To come to the altar with a passion as fire.
To see the family of God grow is her desire.

Watch and see the results of all Hannah's pleas,
Consistently, humbly down on her knees.
Oh, for children to be born in the family of the Lord.
Her praise will be with gladness and adored.

# I'VE LAUNCHED OUT INTO THE DEEP

I came to the Lord one day as I knelt in prayer.
He filled me with the Holy Ghost while kneeling there.
It was a new experience; I'd never felt so close to Him.
I stepped out in to the deep; He was teaching me to swim.

As time went on and I really learned to pray,
That new language took the place of what I had to say.
It seemed nothing else existed; earthly things grew dim.
I'd launched out into the deep; He was teaching me to swim.

Each time the trials come, and things get rough.
I can fall on my knees and that becomes enough.
For it's my secret closet where each battle I can win.
I can launch out into the deep, for He has taught me how to swim.

# LET ME COME INTO YOUR PRESENCE

Let me come into Your presence
Humbly before Thy throne.
Let me come into Your presence
Redeemed as Your own.

Fill me with Your Spirit.
Cover me with Your grace.
Let me come into Your presence
To meet You face to face.

Burdens may seem so heavy,
My eyes may turn away.
Sustained by His Spirit,
At His side I'll stay.

Just a touch of His Spirit
Gladness in my soul.
Safe in His pavilion
Boldly to the throne I go.

I stand before You unworthy
Of all You did for me.
Let Your precious blood.
Cover all my iniquity.

# MAKE AN ALTAR

When I make an altar, I find what God wants me to do.
To be of service to Him that is pure and true.
My heart renders worship honoring Him who is King.
Communion between me and my Lord, my sacrifice I bring.

When I make my altar, I receive the strength for perseverance
For each of my trials I walk, because of Him with endurance.
Assured of who I am in Him, a winner; come what may.
Because I am trusting in each promise that God did say.

When I make my altar, it's then I learn of His power.
I can feel His presence in the midnight hour.
It doesn't matter what others may say or spurn.
I can stand in God's peace; His faithfulness I've learned.

It's the altar where I come so often to seek His face.
I can rest in a peace that passes all understanding and grace.
Because I know that the battle is not mine,
Surrendering my will, allowing Him to shine.

You also can make an altar for rest if you are worn.
This altar will help you find the needed eye of the storm.
You can find what you need and so much more.
Make an altar often and see what He has in store.

# MY PRAYER CLOSET

I had gone to my prayer closet to pray, and the Lord met me there.
He said it's time to clean out my closet of the garments that I wear.
So, we took the time to look at each piece,
whether to keep or reject.
This venture gave me a better understanding of God, and respect.

You must get rid of the heavy coat of sorrow for those rainy days.
I will replace it with Judah's lighter garment, the garment of praise.
Here is the coat of Joseph, which is beautiful with many a hue.
It will remind you of the love and favor I have given to you.

There was the vest that I popped buttons in my sinful conceit,
And He replaced it with Samuel's coat of consecration so meek.
He told me to keep the garment of salvation that I found,
And guard the relationship with Him and a mind so sound.

He showed me the prodigal son's robe his father had for him.
It represented forgiveness, which covered my sin.
He set the garment of righteousness next in line.
He explained the armor for protection and its design.

The accessories in my closet had their purpose, too.
The helmet of salvation and gospel of peace for my shoes.
Don't forget the belt of truth; gird around you tight.
It's important not to lose it, guard it with all your might.

After we had gone over each piece one by one
It was clear what my loving Savior had done.
All these garments and accessories He did bring
So I could be counted worthy to kneel before my King.

# MY SPIRITUAL HAMMOCK

I was so tired and weary, so I decided that I would rest.
I felt I was entitled to this since I had given my best.
Nothing would feel better than to take a little snooze.
I wouldn't be long and really, there was nothing to lose.

I made my way to the storage where my hammock was housed.
I expected that nothing from my nap would be aroused.
Setting up the bunk, adjusting each rope around two trees,
I crawled in the hammock only to fall out on my knees.

Again and again in vain, as hard as I could try,
It only tossed me out again; I began to question why.
This looked so easy, and I've seen others in this lay,
What was wrong with this hammock I had put up today?

I tried once again and found myself sprawled on the ground.
This was harder than a day's work, this falling down.
This hammock looked inviting between these two trees,
But humiliating as I found myself more often on my knees.

I was about to rise to my feet determined not to be defeated.
A lesson was in all these escapades, I finally conceded.
There on my knees I was to find my needed rest.
Prayer was the answer to my anxiety and weariness.

When my feet are tired and my heart is weary, now I know.
I need just a touch of His presence, so to God's throne I go.
I must work with all I have while it is day.
My rest will only be found when I find time to pray.

# OH, BE CAREFUL,
# LITTLE MOUTH, WHAT YOU SAY

Zacharias held the writing tablet and
pen in hand to write his son's name.
Elisabeth had said the baby would be called John;
would he say the same?
The family waited to see if Zacharias would
keep the tradition of generations.
Naming the child after someone in the
domestic line as proper venerations.

Zacharias and Elisabeth were righteous,
walking in all the commandments and ordinances.
They prayed earnestly for a child many years,
still faithful and blameless in their daily onuses.
Elisabeth was barren, and both were now well
stricken in years – way past their prime
Continuing in what they knew, waiting on
God to answer their prayer in His time.

Zacharias was performing his duties of incense
in the temple as the order of his obligations.
When there appeared unto him an angel of the Lord,
with amazing declarations.
And when Zacharias saw him, he was troubled,
and fear fell upon his heart.
But the angel said, Fear not, Zacharias:
for thy prayer is heard and God will impart.

Zacharias said to the angel, Whereby shall I know this?
For I am old, my wife up in years.
The angel said, I am Gabriel, standing in the presence of God;
and speak my words in reveres.

We are told God made Zacharias dumb
and could not speak for God's specific reason.
But would honor and bless him and Elisabeth with every word
at the appointed season.

Sometimes we pray in the will of God,
but our faith wavers before the provision.
So, He has to close our mouths so we don't vacillate,
making the wrong decision
It's in our patience, believing it will be
worth it all when it is accomplished.
God in His mercy guides our speech
so our prayers won't be demolished.

Death and life are in the power of our words,
which can change the course of our mission.
It's important to surround our lives and dreams
with those that will enhance the commission.
God sent Mary to Elisabeth while she carried the
treasure of their lifelong petition.
Mary took this time to help and encourage
Elisabeth with a wonderful rendition.

Thou shalt have joy and gladness and
many shall rejoice at John's birth.
He shall be great and bring praises and honor
 to God in all the earth.
The Spirit will go before him turning the
disobedient to the wisdom of the just.
The two women reveled in the goodness and
wonderful things God did entrust.

Zacharias was dumb for a long time,
but it was to preserve the requested prayer.

So, God did this eccentric thing in order
to make the blessing a perfect affair.
This puts the children's song in a more
significant light and sway.
Remembering in lieu of our prayers, oh,
be careful little mouth, what you say.

Zacharias wrote with pen, His name is John,
which is "gracious" in meaning.
Indeed, God had been gracious, and all
praised the Lord, their hearts singing.
We may have to hold our tongues in the interim,
we may greatly ponder,
While God, in His own timing,
will bring it to pass for His glory and honor.

# FAR BEYOND RUBIES

# AFAR OFF

Peter kept his distance, hiding in the crowd
Or behind a building or two.
The soldiers had come for Jesus,
And he wondered what they would do.
He mingled in the crowd:
"You're Jesus' disciple, with him you've dined."
But fear gripped his heart,
He swore, and vulgarly the fact declined.
As the cock crowed that morn,
He remembered the words Jesus spoke.
He ran afar off, for it was then his heavy heart broke.

Following close, we may have to go through a trial,
Up Golgotha's Hill,
But we will experience
The great resurrection and His eminence reveal.
It will be worth all the things that we've gone through
To see heaven,
That wonderful place that He's prepared for you.
So, stay close to Him
And never let go of His nail-scarred hand.

For He will never be afar off,
If for Him, we will stand.
He's promised never to leave
Or forsake you regardless of your load.
Just cling to Him and He'll help
You walk down life's road.

# A FATHER'S BLESSING

Jacob and Esau desired the blessing of their father,
coveting its worth.
Then came the day Isaac was ready to
give birthright before leaving this earth.
But in their thoughtless moments a deal
would change their lives for years,
Cause a heart wrenching schism filled with misery and tears.

A young man or lady today still finds it
challenging to follow what their father holds.
Not understanding their father's statutes
and often not heeding what they are told.
Oh, for the understanding of a father in the
home living in the love of the Lord.
The abundant blessings that can flow
for generations to come is theirs to afford.

God gave the fathers a command to
be the priest of the home and kin,
To direct his children and family to
keep the ways of the Lord and not sin.
He lives and instructs what is right and just,
making an altar before his King,
Praying to purify his home so they honor
and glory to Jesus bring.

A father tirelessly provides for his household
as God's strength permits.
He cares his child is faltering and
offers his resources to his limits.
Protecting his own as God shows guidance for the trials ahead,
He prayerfully forges the path by which his family is led.

The delight of a father is children
following the statutes put in place.
This brings a sweet peace that hardship
or trials cannot erase.
Great is the pleasure when obedience
according to all written in God's plan,
Bringing blessings, honor and good
success are in the father's hand.

# BETWEEN THE PROMISE
# AND THE PROVISION

Jacob had been promised to be the father of many nations.
Now standing obscurely with his brother's intimidations,
He wrestled with the problem, trying to get some rest.
God had promised, but could the situation stand the test?

Wrestling from dusk until the dawn of light,
Jacob wouldn't let go though he lost the fight.
I won't let you go until you bless me thorough.
Little did he know the transformation on the morrow.

God not only changed his name but his gait,
Teaching him to slow down and learn to wait.
His attitude was altered for the difficulty in store,
Now an assurance in his soul as never before

We may not understand why the pain or doubt,
But we have a promise that He would bring us out.
It's hard to press on while holding the promise assured,
When the way for the provisions seems to be obscured.

Slow down in the confusion and pain to see God's design.
Look for the blessing that He has for you to find.
You will come forth as pure gold as you press in His will.
There are greater things coming as your heart is still.

You will not be the same as before the battle began;
His blessing will empower you for a greater plan.
Changing your name and giving you authority renowned
To be all He wants you to be where abundant life is found.

# COMPLETE IN CHRIST

Failure seemed to be my plight with the struggle I faced.
I stumbled with each step, finding no solid place.
Oh! To feel confident in the task I had started.
The perfecting of this child had surely departed.
All I must do is call on His precious name.

An unkind word pierced my heart with distress,
Welling up anger, hate and unrighteousness.
This is not what children of God deserve.
How can an individual have such a nerve?
Complete in His forgiveness, He took control.

Life was going so well when things came to an abrupt stop.
I found myself on my face, the biggest "Ker-plop."
Then I realized I had made the wrong turn.
This was God's way of helping me to learn.
My thoughts and ways are not as pure as He,
But complete in His wisdom, I can trust Him confidently.

Complete in Christ, you find restful peace
As each day passes that will increase.
Covered by the blood of the precious Lamb,
In the name of Jesus, His child I am.
The struggle of this flesh is so cheaply priced
When I fully live a life complete in Christ.

# I MISSED YOU TODAY

You arose from your bed after a good night's rest,
Took a few extra minutes to dress to look your best,
Picked up your belongings, made sure you had your keys,
You remembered everything but falling to your knees.

I provided sunshine, and the roads were fine.
The traffic was heavy, then you began to whine.
"I'm going to be late; I've rushed to be on time.
Aha, the toll road," reaching for a dollar and dime.

Lunch time came; you rushed in line to order your meal,
Put change in the pop machine, then turned on your heel.
Sat down to eat, savoring the warmth of the garlic bread,
Delved into your meal without bowing your head.

People came and went as you worked through the day.
You took time to converse, and appreciation convey.
Busily making sure all the proper work was done,
So, at quitting time, you once again were on the run.

Finally, when you were home and your time was your own,
You put your keys away and dialed the phone.
Later in the evening, you sat to watch the news,
Nodding your head, you decided it was time to snooze.

So, you arose to get ready for bed,
Crawled in and laid down your weary head.
It wasn't long before you had fallen asleep.
Then that's when My heart began to weep.

All those precious things that I would have lovingly shared,
That I love you and brought to your attention I really cared.
But you didn't stop to take the time to read or pray.
Somehow, I must make you understand, I missed you today.

# I'M COVERED

Although the battle rages all around me
Waves surround beyond what I can see.
Fear tries to grip my heart and mind,
But I'm not moved by what I find.

I don't understand why things come my way,
Nor know how long this adversity will stay.
I may be tossed to and fro, my faith tested.
But in His confidence, oh, soul be thou rested.

He is my fortress, my shield and buckler strong.
In Him I'm safe for however this adversity is long.
The tempest may rage; my world comes crashing down.
You are my Rock, my solace and safety in You I've found.

I whisper and know You will answer my call.
Be my horn, let Your Spirit and anointing fall.
I stand in awe; light of Your countenance upon me.
You cover me with Your feathers, with excellency.

# IN THE TIME OF HARVEST

It was time to obtain the promised land,
thus Joshua gave instructions mightily sober.
Coming to Jordan at the time of harvest,
Israel lodged there before crossing over.
They were to follow the ark,
so they would know the way
by which they must go,
For they had not passed this way before,
but God's presence would show.

And Joshua said to the people,
Sanctify yourselves for the days ahead,
For tomorrow the Lord will do wonders
among you just as He had said.
The Lord promised Joshua He would
exalt and be with him as he obeyed,
Giving him and the children of Israel
victory as the directions conveyed.

Joshua said, "By this you shall know
that the living God is among you,
He will without fail drive out your
enemies greatly from before you."
The people did as Joshua commanded,
following God's demonstration
Of His wisdom, protection,
and power in colossal revelation.

We find ourselves standing at our
Jordan at the time of harvest, intimidated,
But our Jordan is God opportunity
for His power to be demonstrated.
It's then we must sanctify ourselves and
find God's presence and divinity,

Following God's Word that we know in
our hearts and stand in His authority.
God gives us an assignment which He can help us get through.
We try to avoid it or find a way that will be the easiest to do.
There is a time of cleansing and
sanctification before we can start
Getting in God's presence to find what is God's will and heart.
There are times we need His power
to take authority over the problem,
Or just give it to God for the solution,
knowing He can solve them.

# PRICELESS

A shekel of silver, an ounce of gold,
An American dollar, it's not to be sold.
This peace, satisfaction, a contentment of mind,
Wisdom, love, understanding, joy sublime
Exchanged for a car, home, or bank account.
Sorry, no exchange for this great flowing fount.
Humble, repentant, fully surrender.
Soul! That's what it takes to reach that splendor.

# SHAKE OFF THE DUST

As we live each day, life doesn't always go as planned.
We tend to get discouraged and want to hide in the sand.
Our first thought is to look at ourselves as failed in our toil.
We want to just quit or propose that area of our lives to recoil.

We find failure being as an undertaker rather than our teacher.
We may be created of dust, but in God, far from a frail creature.
We forget that failure is for just a moment, a diminutive time.
It's not as degrading as we thought; it's not always a negative sign.

God is our strength in the time of weakness, His grace all we need.
Our failure is just one more lesson, a steppingstone as God leads.
Failure brings us to the foot of the cross as before Him we kneel,
The time to find the "perfect place" in
His power and wondrous will.

There is winsome freedom in the
person who will shake off the dust,
Shake off the failure of his life and freely in God put his trust.
The total confidence in Christ with overcoming adoration
Gives a dust-free lifestyle of perfect hope and reconciliation.

Shake the dust off your feet; live for the forthcoming days.
Forget the past and commit to God all your ways.
Never give up or you'll never reach your potential.
In God, you will find His strength is the only essential.

# THE PROCESS TO THE PROMISE

When one receives a promise, they oft expect it right away.
They are filled with anticipation for the appointed day.
One thing we know, we can be assured,
God's Word is "yea and amen."
But His timing is not ours and can be "not right now," but then
The journey to our promise can detour
our plans, hopes or dreams.
Yet God's promises are for sure
and will happen when He deems.

Abraham was promised that his seed
would be as abundant as the sand.
In the wait, he and Sarah thought
they would help God out with His plan.
Abraham's nurturing of Lot and Ishmael
got God's attention through the years.
But this was not God's promise, and brought many tears.
Abraham learned to wait on God to receive the promised son,
Accepting the Lord's timing and will to be done.

Joseph had a dream that he a great leader would be.
But little did he understand the ups
and downs in life he would see.
Betrayed by his brothers, sold as slave, imprisoned by a lie,
Although he found favor with the prison guard,
still wondered why.
Through all the trials that put his life in an unusual whirl
God made him the person to preserve his known world.

When the Children of Israel left Egypt,
God promised a special land,
But their faith wavered and they doubted His command.

The river of Jordan between them and Canaan,
an army rushing from behind,
They were in a frenzy with the situation
and wanted everything to resign.
With the encouragement of Moses,
they moved forward to see
The Lord perform a mighty miracle
as they crossed the Red Sea.

Ruth learned to love Naomi's God and
longed to see the land in which she lived.
She hoped for a better life to see what
Naomi's God could do or give.
A journey took her to a path of
obedience and instruction each day.
Following the words of her mother-in-law,
learning the Israelite way.
Ruth's dedication to do what she was told
and humble herself the path to glean
Brought the best of the promise to marrying
the richest man of that day ever seen.

The servants of the Cana wedding were given
unusual instructions for promise of wine.
This task was mundane and so ridiculous,
gathering all the pots they could find.
They went to the river or well, wherever they
found water to collect.
But it was still water regardless of the amount -
just as before they would inspect.
Back and forth pouring repeatedly, still not s
eeing the promise in the task
They followed, nevertheless, the instruction
they had been asked.

Jacob knew the promise of being a great nation,
but he had a great flaw.
His name meant "deceiver" and he had
an issue with his wayward brother Esau.
He battled within himself, but finally
went to sleep on a stone on the ground.
That's where God met him with a blessing
 that was greatly profound.
It was a battle with God's angel not only
changed his character but his posture.
He was changed inside and out, assured of
 God's promise and future.

God has many promises for us today;
we can have each and every one.
But the process to those assurances has
a journey that we tend to shun.
There is a time of waiting or trials of
ups and downs through our life.
We tend to lose the promise because of
wrongs and unexpected strife.
But God is there to encourage us
and help us to follow His instruction.
Through the mundane things of life
or needed spiritual construction

Yes, we can have all the promises, all of them are ours,
But it's the process that we must go through we think devours.
But not really, God just getting us
ready so we can handle the gift.
We are groomed and fitted for the
ability to shine with His lift.
This process is the kind that changes
us to make the diamond shine,

To make us His treasure with His
anointing and power divine.

# THROUGH HIS EYES

Sometimes I fail, trying to do my best.
No matter what, I seem to fail the test.
I make a mess, in my trying still,
Attempting to live in God's perfect will.

He must increase as my will I surrender.
His Word declares He's my Rock and defender.
I can have and can be all His Word affords,
When looking through the eyes of the Lord.

I read that I fell short of what He wants for me.
But, oh, Love and Grace is what I see.
I may not be all that I want or should.
But I read He has my future, and all is good.

My fear is replaced with peace beyond the knowing.
Unbelief is erased by His greatness unfolding.
My weakness is hidden in His strength divine,
As His righteousness, favor, and blessings are made mine

It's only as I walk in His word and the excellence of His power
He perfects me for His work, minute by minute, hour by hour.
So now I look at what He said I am as I abide in Him
Rather than see the wretched life that is produced by sin.

I can do all that is expected and planned for me,
Because His word has said it and has given the power to be.
Walking with confidence knowing whatever in the future lies
I can have a great outlook on life looking through His eyes.

# WHAT'S IMPORTANT

I've never had the privilege to sit on the Supreme Court
Nor sit at a table with a king of a nation.
I've never sailed to a faraway port,
Nor given impressive words of proclamation.

I may not have the wisdom to advise the Secretary of State
Or be a king of a foreign land.
But I can be confident of my fate,
Because I'm following my Father's plan.

I have felt the presence of my Heavenly Father's love,
Communed with Him in an intimate way.
He has given me His power from above.
This King walks with me each moment of the day.

With all this in mind, I've been made to realize
It's not what or who we are down here,
But just to be God's and righteous in His eyes
Then that's when this life becomes clear.

# YOUR VALUE

Someone may be tall and look good to the eye,
Then there are those that are short or just a bit shy.
One may be a politician, lawyer, doctor, or preacher,
Or they could be a plumber, cashier, or a teacher.

We all are different in color, culture, and attributes,
Each having a gift that the other needs and contributes.
If we were all one thing in this life, having no diversity,
We would lack some necessities, which causes perplexity.

There are many things in this life we regard with great merit.
It may cost us a price or something that we may inherit.
We differ in opinion of what is important or hold in esteem,
But we must not forget we are children of the King.

Our value is not the position we hold nor clothes we wear,
But the fact that we are God's child; we are His heir.
An item is treasured when one learns the creator's identity.
This determines an item's value because of the authenticity.

Whether we seem insignificant or influential to those around
We all have equal importance regardless of our background.
Earthly value cannot be measured by a monetary evaluator.
Our true value or worth is found in Jesus Christ, our Creator.

# FINDING TREASURE

# ABIDING IN HIM

As I read my Bible, purge me with Your word.
Make it a part of my life; let my heart be stirred.
Renew me with Your presence, each day afresh,
In a way as to walk in the Spirit and not in the flesh.

Help me to abide in Your Will as Your Word makes it known,
Abiding in Your anointing that You place on Your own.
I, as a branch grafted in You, the vine,
Help me be unseen by the world and only Jesus find.

# DRAW IT OUT OF ME

God allowed Moses to be drawn out of the waters of the Nile,
To be nurtured by Pharaoh's daughter,
refined by God all the while.
Moses grew, making it hard to keep
quiet his purpose of God's plan.
Therefore, God drew him from the
water to the palace of Pharaoh's land.

God changed his surroundings to
prepare him for righteous dictate,
Drawing him from rags to riches,
from family to affairs of state.
A new level beyond the norm,
he'd outgrown his modest place.
Greater tasks and elevation lay
ahead for Moses to face.

There are wonderful ideas and dreams that are not revealed,
Hidden in the secret depths of each of our souls still concealed.
We get restless and wonder, what is God's will for our life.
We can't hide it anymore, thinking our anxiety is strife.

It's coming out in a way that we don't want to transpire,
Trying to do for God, searching for His favor and anointing fire.
It's time to decide "What I am is not what I want to be"
And let God do the work so that we can be completely free.

Let God draw out of us those gifts
and dreams to enlarge our territory,
And live in His anointing, the abundant
life extraordinary.
Allow Him to draw out the gifts moment
by moment, hour by hour
As we live a life expecting a new level, inhabiting His power,

# GARDENER OR MASTER

Mary Magdalene may have seen the children on Jesus' knee,
Heard of the large net of fishes wrought from Galilee.
She may have been told of the turning water into wine,
And saw the widow with the mite standing in line.

Mary may have sat and listened to the lessons Jesus taught,
Experienced the miracle of the five loaves the little lad brought.
It was no doubt in her mind that Jesus really cared
For all the wonderful works and love that He shared.

But the day that He forgave her of all her sin,
She no longer saw Him as a gardener, but a friend.
True, He took care of those He touched each day.
Now she had a love for Him in a special way.

There in the garden to the tomb Mary came,
She then understood as Jesus called her name.
Jesus was no longer just the gardener, serving her needs.
But she was to be the servant, falling to her knees.

She now could acknowledge him as Master and Lord,
He, being the one to be served and adored.
So today meet Him at the tomb and listen for His call,
No longer a gardener of your life, but as Master of all.

# THE RIGHT OF PASSAGE

The Children of Israel stood at the Red Sea's shore,
Waiting to proceed into the promised land to wander no more.
Moses stretched his rod over the
waters for them to pass through,
Obeying the word God had commanded him to do.

We, the children of God,
have not the blessings that could be ours,
But we are now standing at Jordan's shores lacking the power.
God has given us the right of heaven's blessings if we believe
And expect what God said was ours if we would receive.

He gives us the right of passage to
cross over to claim what we need.
Whether salvation or healing, we ought not to plead.
His Word teaches we should come boldly to His throne
With the faith of a child, we who are His own.

We need to find our place in God that we can live in His anointing
With each step of our lives with a divine appointing,
Walking confidently each day through any test
Because it is in God, our faith we fully rest.

# STIR UP THE ANOINTING

The celebration was in its third day in Cana of Galilee,
A festivity of eating and drinking for every attendee.
Jesus and His disciples were invited to this event.
Everything was going fine until all the wine was spent.

Mary, the mother of Jesus, approached Jesus about the situation.
The wine is gone, and the wedding has more days of celebration.
Jesus didn't seem to be interested as He answered in displeasure.
But she was confident He would do
the right thing at her conjecture.

There was a rare relationship between the mother and Son.
She had seen him grow and knew His purpose was to come.
Her expectation was a nudge of
the power that He had detained,
Her prodding was stirring the anointing He secretly contained.

Fill the water pots with water, Jesus gave the command.
So, the servants filled the six pots to the brim by hand.
Draw out now and bear unto the governor of the affair.
The best wine was now ready for all to share.

Only the servants knew what miracle had just taken place.
The pots made after the manner of Jewish purifying grace,
A vessel for holding water for
cleansing or oil for household customs.
Now there was abundant wine in the vessels,
an impracticable sum.

We are called vessels that God longs to fill with his Spirit and Love,
With a new wine, talked about in the book of Acts, from above.
He cleanses your vessel and fills it with the incense so sweet.
As we submit ourselves to do His will, humbly and complete.

It's a hallowed experience as
He seals us with this wonderful assurance,
Destroying the yoke of sin, giving healing and strong endurance.
This anointing will guide you and teach you all truths.
It's holy and is the center of praise, all discouragement defuse.

The request Mary asked of Jesus was a
call for Him to stir up His anointing.
She knew why He came and what
was encouraging His appointing.
His response seemed that He had disapproval and hesitation,
But she prodded with her words for
the servants to give observation.

As a Spirit-filled vessel, we often sit
on the appointment God has given.
We are hesitant to follow His bidding
and our call is deeply hidden.
What will our family say or what if I try and completely fail?
We are fearful of what others will say and the nay-sayer's rail.

Now is the time to stir up what God has put in our hearts.
Ask for the courage to increase with strength to do our part.
Search your heart and stir up the gift that you have received.
He's given you the power as His Word you believed.

Stir up the anointing as it will guide you as He opens gates.
Submit yourself to His will and follow His precious mandates.
His anointing will be your companion and diminish your fall
As we submit to His will and follow His gentle call.

# SUPPER IS ENDED

Jesus had walked with His disciples and taught them each day.
He knew of their shortcomings
and loved them as they were anyway.
When His time had come to give His life,
the purpose for which He came,
He prepared a meal for the last time;
His Father's words proclaim.

As supper ended, He laid aside the coat that He wore,
Picked up a towel and water in a basin He did pour.
He stooped down to wash each of the disciples' feet.
As an example of humility, He did entreat.

The Lord walks with us and knows all the time we waver.
Lovingly He watches, keeping us; remember, He's the Savior.
We have come into His house and
feasted on the meal He has prepared.
But it's time to lay aside the garment of slothfulness and care.

It's high time to pick up the towel, for the supper is long spent.
The call was given, and we've forgotten the commission to be sent.
Arise and hasten, seize the towel that is assigned to you,
For God has given a work for each one of us to do.

# THE CHILDREN OF GOD

God's Word was given that our joy would be complete,
Declaring that God is light; in Him there is no defeat.
We walk in the light as He shows us the way,
Having fellowship and communion with Him each day.

Confessing our sin because He's faithful and true,
Buried with Him in baptism and filled with His Spirit, too.
Christ is the propitiation for our sin
And will perfect us as He abides within.

We become strong as we live according to His Word,
Walking in the truth which we have heard,
Children of God who abide in His anointing power,
Living unashamed and confident each day and hour.

Loving our brother while here down on earth,
Spreading the precious gospel of the new birth,
Occupying until we reach our primary goal:
To be with Jesus, the One who saved our soul.

# TREASURES IN EARTHEN VESSELS

Let me be a lump of clay in the Potter's hand
To be molded and used in God's perfect plan.
Make me a vessel that Your glory will shine through,
Available and worthy to put Your spirit into.

Let this treasure take control of my life each day,
Be a beacon for those who stumble along the way.
Stooped, bowed down in despair, will no longer fear,
Their hearts will have hope and see You clear.

This peace You put in me, may it ever be found,
When the storms are raging, and clouds are all around.
Others may know that it's a far greater power,
In this vessel abiding during the midnight hour.

Oh, that the joy and happiness that You did impart
Be a salve, an ointment to a deep hurting heart.
Put in an excellent spirit to worship and sing,
A vessel of glory and honor for the Master bring.

Let this treasure in my earthen vessel overflow,
And not be hidden from those who do not know.
Let Your Spirit work and have full reign,
So someone else can likewise this treasure gain.

# REACHING
# HEAVEN'S GATES

# DOESN'T ANYBODY WANT TO GO TO HEAVEN?

Doesn't anybody want to go to Heaven anymore,
Where the gates are made of pearl?
Doesn't anybody want to walk to Heaven anymore,
Instead of the way of the world?

Doesn't anybody want to look for Heaven anymore,
To the city where Jesus is the light?
Doesn't anybody strive for Heaven anymore,
We'll be given robes of pure white?

Doesn't anybody long to go to Heaven anymore,
Where we'll dine with the Lamb?
Isn't anybody excited going to Heaven anymore,
We'll spend eternity with the Great I AM!

# GOD'S GREAT ARMS

My son, I forgot the pain of birth when they laid you in my arms.
Your every cry and movement enchanted me with utmost charm.
You were so precious and dependent on me for your every need.
Each day I felt you were a rare treasure from God, yes indeed.

As you grew, sometimes falling, becoming bruised along the way,
I would be there with arms outstretched no matter the time or day.
No matter what the bumps were in the road for you as a child,
I could put my arms around you and
tried so hard things to reconcile.

God saw fit to let you grow into a
young man with a heart of concern,
But there was one hard lesson as a mother I had to learn.
My arms could not reach to every path that you wish to trod,
So those were the times I had to leave
the out-stretched arms to God.

As I stand before you, today is one
those times I'm unable to achieve
That hug I long to give you so for all your heartaches to relieve.
Now I will commit you to God's care and ask this one favor:
That He will keep us both until we stand
together before our Savior.

Until then may He hold us both in
His arms with you there and me here,
For the pain is great and may linger
for some time, for you're so dear.
I know your place is far greater than
where I am at this present time.
It's a comfort for me to know His
arms are far stronger than mine.

# IF IT HADN'T BEEN FOR
# THE NEIGHBOR NEXT DOOR

An invitation to go to church was extended to me.
I really didn't know how important it could be.
My outlook on life would have never changed,
If it hadn't been for the neighbor next door.

I felt the presence of God in the service I attended.
I chose to sit by a dear saint, hands to God extended.
I would have never received my blessing,
If it hadn't been for the neighbor next door.

Each one's life influences someone near.
Consequently, live a life diligently and without fear,
Of hearing "I wouldn't be lost
If it hadn't been for the neighbor next door."

But rather, with hand in hand with each new day
Bind together, uplift and encourage along the way,
To hear, "I wouldn't have made it,
If it hadn't been for the neighbor next door."

# THE CHOSEN PATH

Each of us has a decision of which path of life to pursue.
Your choice has been the pathway that God desired for you.
The road has not been easy, but He has always been by your side.
He's been that companion in which you could assuredly confide.

There were times the road was too rugged,
 so you've stopped to rest.
But "Get back up," has been your motto,
"With God's help to pass the test."
The smooth path filled your life with delightful praise and song.
Then was the time you found the
strength to help someone else along.

Whether the sun shone or rain beat down slowing your pace,
Your goal was constant – to see the blessed Master's face.
In any case, the path led up
the mountain and in the lowest of hollow
Your footprints are assuredly left for your posterity to follow.

You may not know what this life's journey holds just ahead,
But you still have the same faithful Lord who has already led
You down the road that will life's ebb and flow unfold.
Be assured the cobblestone path becomes the road of gold.

# WE'RE NOT HOME YET

We live as though our eternity is going to be spent on this Earth
Allowing the fleeting to override the eternal, we often forget,
Planning our lives according to our temporal self-worth.
We're just pilgrims and strangers here; we're not home yet.

Troubles come and we wonder why things are going wrong.
We look to others expecting to have all our needs met.
There is a sadness in our heart, we've lost our song.
Remember, this world is not our home; we're not home yet.

Loved ones pass on to the other side, leaving us behind.
We take  into account the individual's worth or net,
The accomplishments and good characteristics we can find.
What's done for Christ will last while we're not home yet.

This earth that we live in is just a dressing room,
Preparing us for the supper table that God has set.
Anxiously awaiting the marriage to the Bridegroom,
This is our greatest hope, even though we're not home yet.

# GOD HAS GIVEN
# US LEADERSHIP

# HEARTBEAT OF A SHEPHERD

As the praises are ringing and service begins,
The shepherd watches the flock coming in.
All through the service, he takes note of who is there.
Although a smile on his face, his heart is in despair.
There is a sheep missing, with a heart forlorn,
Is his sheep in the thicket, caught and torn?

Through prayer and fasting, he gets a word from the Lord.
His heart is burning with the wisdom he's explored.
Baring his soul, feeding the flock with spiritual instruction,
Reaching out to those who are lost, heading for destruction.
Nurturing his precious flock in God's Word,
His greatest joy is when God's truth is gird.

The shepherd shares the joyous times as well as the bad,
Joining in the laughter or crying tears with the sad.
Praising the Lord with those who are blessed,
Encouraging that one who is going through a test.
All are his sheep, in whatever condition they're found,
His greatest concern, the Holy Ghost does abound.

He knows that the flock will make it through.
If he can help them understand what God wants to do
Is molding their lives into the Master's plan.
Then the shepherd before God and judgment stand,
Declaring, "Father, I've pastored as diligently as I know how.
Into Your care I place this precious flock now."

# OUR PASTOR

The shepherd of Lighthouse calls each of his sheep by name.
It's so amazing he remembers, no matter how many have came.
Guiding the flock in paths that lead in the way of God's provisions,
Leaning on the Lord for each step to make the right decisions.
He feeds his flock and, in his prayers, carries them in his soul.

He ministers to the wounded until God makes them whole.
Gently nudging each lamb that seems that wants to stray,
Protecting each of his sheep from the dangers that prey.

His work isn't easy and takes much strength and toil,
As he with his wisdom administers the compassionate oil.
Making sure the sheep are covered with God's anointed power,
Counseling, and praying, the shepherd
labors for many a long hour.

The love for his flock keeps his passion burning anew,
His hopes and dreams are many waiting for God to do.
The road may not be easy, and steep mountains to ascend,
But he follows the Great Shepherd on whom he can depend.

We pray for our shepherd who tends
 the flock faithfully each week.
May God strengthen and keep you
as His face you earnestly seek.
We appreciate the example of love,
compassion, and determination.
May our love for the Savior meet
your hopes and expectations.

# OUR PASTOR'S WIFE

She rings the phone, "Honey, when can I expect you so I can
have dinner on the table?"
On the other end comes the reply,
"Go ahead and eat; I'll be there when I'm able. "
The sink is stopped, and the dishwasher
can't run without being fixed soon.
Neither can she do the clothes, as the
washer backs up later that afternoon.

She has loved being a Godly example
and mother to children of her own,
And come to find a place in her heart
for our children, the love has grown.
As the head of the Sunday School,
her greatest desire on this earth is to win;
Each young child that comes to church
allows God to cleanse him from sin.

It's quite interesting to watch the pastor's wife from her pew.
You can usually know what stories the pastor is telling are true.
However it may seem that she is in the background of things,
She is always busy with something, with whatever her life brings.

Waiting and changing her plans is an
art she learned early in their ministry years,
For she never can keep up with her
husband's fast paced, ever-changing gears.
So, we would like to take a moment
just to say for all that goes unobserved
A great big "Thank you" and we love
you with the honor you long deserved.

# SALVATION

# CALVARY STILL FLOWS

Falling on His face, "Father, take this cup from Me."
Groanings from His soul, "Nevertheless, not My will."
Thorns on His brow, stripes on His back
O what love for me!
Love that caused Calvary to flow.

Kneeling in Your presence, have mercy on me.
From the depths of my heart, use me as You will.
Heal all my pain,
Make me anew
As only You can do.
Cover me with the Calvary flow.

His love still reaches with amazing grace.
His blood washes whiter than snow.
The nails He bore in heaven reserve me a place.
All because Calvary still flows.

# COME TO JESUS

There's a longing in your heart.
You can't fill it.
The hurting heart you have
You can't conceal it.
You're filled with gloom,
For God's there's no room,
You need life anew.
Let me tell you what to do.
Come to Jesus.

Now there's a song in your heart.
You can sing it.
There's assurance in His word.
You can believe it.
You can hold to His hand.
By His side you can stand
You can gladly sing.
Let His high praises ring.
Come to Jesus.

Come to Jesus
And let Him fill your emptiness.
Give Him your broken heart and confess.
Here I am,
Lord, I need You,
Give me life anew.
He's waiting for you.
Come to Jesus

# FOLLOW

I can still hear the scraping of the cross up Golgotha's hill
Making a path for us to follow even today, if we will.
A narrow way to salvation if we choose to sojourn,
Or do we pursue the miracles and wonders we've learned?

Some followed Jesus because it was the happenin' thing,
Just to see what wonders and miracles the day would bring.
There were those who made it their way of living,
Not just to receive that day what Jesus was giving.

Do we love Him? Have we really counted the cost?
Or do we follow Him for fear of being lost?
Oh, that we can follow Him because of a love that is real,
Not for society or man's approval or appeal.

Let us search our hearts for which category we fall in.
I don't want to follow Him with a heart full of sin.
But let there be a clean heart that's full of love,
That I can be ready for the place He prepared up above.

# HARVEST IS COMPLETE

We have been sowers of the seed in many years past,
With the Gospel, the only thing in anyone's life that will last.
Whatever means or inspiration with the greatest compassion,
Presenting a timeless message in a timely fashion.

Our faithful efforts of love with much prayer and toil
Fell on all kinds of ground, both rocky and fertile soil.
Some were receptive and others rejected this Word.
We did our part by making sure the message was heard.

We have come this far, enjoying the Lord's merciful hand,
But there is still much to do until before Him we stand.
God has been faithful, as we have served in His field,
Honoring our labor of love, giving us much yield.

But the work is not done; we can't sit at the supper table yet,
Because there are many lost souls that Christ hasn't met.
Rise, and pick up the sickle. We must gather the wheat,
Until we hear the Lord say, "The Harvest is complete!"

# HE'S THE ONE

Far in the garden Jesus fell on His face bowed with grief,
With the sin of the world on His shoulders, He found no relief.
Even though this was His purpose at this time to fulfill,
He cried, "Let this cup pass from Me, nevertheless, not My will."
As Jesus arose to admonish His disciples of temptations persuade
Judas, followed by a crowd, marched into the garden where
Jesus prayed.
"It is He whom I kiss," Judas said.
And when it was done the crowd seized Jesus.
They knew He was the one.

Once in Pilate's court, the ruler gave the crowd a choice to make.
Who would they that  he would release unto them?
Was it a mistake?
"Give us Barabbas!" they cried,
"Release him and let him go free."
"Crucify Jesus; crucify Him, this man from Galilee."
Soldiers beat Him, gave Him a robe,
a crown of thorns for His head,
Gave Him a cross to carry up to Calvary's hill, the crowd led.
At the end of a long night's test, people jeered,
thinking they'd won,
Not knowing that it was He who God had chosen.
Jesus was the one.

Just as Mary and her friends on the
way to the tomb pondered the great stone,
They knew it was a problem none of
them could resolve on their own.
So today we have someone that goes
before to help us with each test.
We need to repent. With a clean heart, serve Him with our best.
Nobody loves you like Jesus, or can cleanse you from within.

The love and mercy shown at Calvary is what saves you from sin.
Your redemption is waiting; with Jesus the work's already done.
He is alive and victorious over Satan and sin.
He is the One!

# I'VE GOT A NEW LIFE

I've got a new life
Since Jesus took control.
I've got a new life
Since He saved my soul.
He took those chains that bound me.
He gave me the victory.
I've got a new life,
Since Jesus took control.

# JESUS' KINGDOM

Jesus came unto the Earth
Through a low and humble birth.
No kingly throne to call His own,
For His kingdom wasn't of this world.

Oh, His kingdom, unlike most,
Was joy in the Holy Ghost,
Bidding all to wait for Pentecost.
His kingdom was in the hearts of men.

It is still for us today.
Poured out in the same unique way.
Repentance, buried in Jesus' name,
Forsaking the kingdoms of this world.

My kingdom's not of the world, Jesus did say.
Make Him your choice, do it today!
The Holy Ghost is for you,
Repent and be baptized, too.
Be ready for His coming today.

# JUDGMENT CALLED, BUT MERCY ANSWERED

Judgment summoned me to his court for the wrongs I had done,
Reading all the charges, naming them one by one.
Glaring down at me he cried, "What are you going to plea?"
My head bowed in shame, it looked hopeless for me.

Each count that had been read, I was guilty as charged.
My sentence, offense by offense, Judgment enlarged.
Standing before the bench without representation for my defense
After swift deliberation the jury resolved
the measure of my recompense.

The verdict was handed down. Mercy stood, demanding,
"Throw out the case.
Each charge that was read, no matter how great, must be erased."
I turned around, confused, to observe
my advocate with great relief.
"Who was my defender?  How could this be?"
I inquired with disbelief!

Mercy pleaded my cause, confirmed the debt had been paid.
Jesus' shed blood on Calvary's cross was how my bail was made.
I'm glad long ago in God's courtroom
my case was already heard.
When Judgments calls, thank God, Mercy answers.
"It's written in God's Word!"

# LEAVE YOUR NETS

Jesus bade His disciples "Come unto me.
Leave your nets, I have work for thee."
They left their vessels and nets at His word,
Pricked in their heart, they were stirred.

They saw His miracles, all the marvelous things,
Listened to wisdom and heard His teachings.
But when the way was treacherous and rough
They went back to their nets, saying, "That's enough."

After His crucifixion Jesus revealed His concern in depth,
Reminding them the importance of commitments kept,
Assuring each that His power was sufficient for each minute,
Giving them instructions for the battle and how to win it.

Even now in this day in which we live,
We try to Him our all to give.
Our hearts seem so willing to do His will.
Here I am, my cup You can fill.

When things come along we don't understand,
We find ourselves heading back to the sand.
We reach once more for the things left behind,
Mending the nets until His will to find.

# NO GREATER LOVE

A baby born to a virgin in Bethlehem's plain.
The angels' message was Jesus is His name.
He grew up as a humble carpenter's son
Knowing in His heart the task to be done.

In His youth, He grew in stature and wisdom with God,
While observing and living on this earthly sod.
Baptized by John in the Jordan River
To fulfill righteousness and to deliver.

Tempted in the wilderness, the turning stones into bread.
"Get thee behind me, it is written," He said.
Love drove Him on to the task before Him.
Mankind's outlook was bleak and oh, so dim.

He came to heal the lame from the chair,
The broken-hearted and worried from their care,
Caused the blind to see the light of day,
And rebuke the devil's demons away.

His disciples, whom He loved, were sore afraid,
When the soldiers came after He prayed,
"Father, not My will, but Thine be done."
Love made Him willing, the Wondrous One.

Spat upon, ridiculed, a crown of thorns on His brow,
Smitten and beaten, but Love didn't stop now.
Through pain, hurt, a broken heart for men,
Still Love said, "There must be a redeemer for them."

Nails in His feet, and the cross in the sands,
Blood dripping from his pierced side and His hands,
Yet on the cross, Jesus said, "I forgive."
Still Love said, "Die, so that men can live."

## THE MASTER'S TOUCH

No greater Love can any human compare,
Or even the glory He has prepared for us there.
Victorious over death, hell, and the grave
Love is why you and I can be saved.

# PERFECT FREEDOM

We are privileged to choose where we want to work or play,
Going about our daily tasks each and every day,
Take a stroll, drive the automobile, or ride public transportation.
We are free to decide, for the most part, our daily destination.

It's up to us how we will do in life, whether we will succeed.
No one can stop your progress if you with determination proceed.
We are blessed to be in a place called the "Land of the Free."
With an apathetic heart we experience this great liberty.

We live in a great nation, one that all of us should hold dear.
With all its beauty and grandeur, there is one thing that is clear.
We should thank God for His love and the power of His hand,
That we have the freedom to worship in this great land.

The perfect freedom is that liberty of the soul set free,
Washed by the blood of the Christ who died at Calvary.
No longer a soul burdened down, wrapped in chains of sin,
Perfect freedom is the person who is free from within.

# THE BLIND MEN'S FAITH

Two blind men came to Jesus one day,
Searching for Him, I heard them say:
"We heard Jesus is the one that can heal,
To make us see, we know He will."
When they got to Jesus, He heard their cry
With compassion, He didn't pass them by.
He saw their faith and gave them a touch.
Who else but Jesus could do so much.
He can do the same for me and you.
If we can have the faith, He'll do it for us, too.

# THROUGH THE DOOR

The captain was checking his bill of lading when
He bade his crew to see what was there within
A crate which did not according to the lading score
So, the sailors with hammer and chisel bore.

Finding a small boy, the captain was far from glad.
"Just where did you think you were going, my lad!"
Timidly the lad followed the owner of the ship.
Quietly and frightened on his toes he did tip.

Down below, the captain's wife he did meet.
As the Captain left, she bade him to have a seat.
"My son, just what country was your destination?"
"Oh, to my father's place, my only relation!"

He said hopefully with excitement in his eyes.
"This was my only chance," he said with a sigh.
The captain's wife said to him, "Let me to you talk.
Don't you think it's better through the door one should walk?

Instead in a crate, for days without something to eat.
Talk to the Captain and make reservations complete.
A bell boy, potato peeler, anything one could have been.
You wouldn't have an angry Captain," she said with a grin.

That's the way many people the Good Captain do.
Just come aboard the Good Captain's ship "according to you."
But this isn't the policy of any vessel to board.
Our way and the Good Captain's way must be in one accord.

That is being on His bill of lading, life's Book of the Lamb.
Come through the word and Jesus, the great I Am.
We must go through the door in the Good Captain's name.
So, at the end of the voyage,
we can stand before Him without shame.

# WHAT WOULD JESUS THINK?

What did Jesus think as He stood in Pilate's hall accused?
Could He see the hearts of all those that abused?
What did Jesus think as stripes on His back were laid?
Was He sure this was the way sickness was to be paid?

What did Jesus think when mocked by the crowd?
He could have stopped them, but He stood with head bowed.
What did Jesus think as the crown of thorns was put on His head?
His authority was powerful, but He stood and bled.

What did Jesus think as on Him they laid a purple cloth?
Did the pain of the open wounds make Him wroth?
What did Jesus think as He carried the cross to Calvary?
Was His heart heavier than the rugged tree?

What did Jesus think as they drove the nails in His hands?
He could have been rescued just by a command.
What did Jesus think as He hung between
heaven and Earth's plain?
He loved those, His accusers, heaven's portal to gain.

What does Jesus think when we have a Pilate's heart?
We have nothing to do with the Lord, or maybe just part?
What does Jesus think when He offers us a crown?
Not this way of life, so we turn it down.

What about the robe of pure white?
Do we open the wounds again, not me, not tonight!
Do we place the nails over again as we look at Calvary?
Do we impose those nails with our actions, "Prove it to me"?

What does Jesus think as we put Him back on trial?
As you're coming up with your verdict, He's waiting while
You finally find the case has been closed and won.
God has granted the power for you to become His son.

# WHICH SIDE OF THE CROSS?

Our Lord hung on the cross for the sins of everyone.
He surrendered His will until our salvation was done.
That day He hung on the cross between two thieves.
They represent those who do and don't believe.

The thief on the right believed Jesus' message of love,
Requesting of Him to forgive and receive him above.
Jesus, in the hour so dark, granted this sinner's petition,
Granting him a place in His Kingdom due to his contrition.

On the other hand, the thief on the left scorned and railed.
Whatever Jesus' purpose was it had surely failed.
"If you be the Christ, save yourself and prove your power."
His disdain showed his disbelief in his dismal hour.

Each sinner made the choice for his own destination,
By choosing or rejecting the Lord's salvation.
We, today, have the option on each side of the cross
We can doubt or believe, having life or being lost.

The choice of salvation still echoes through ages of time.
What is your choice? Which side of the cross will you find?
On the right, believing gives life in abundance anew,
Or on the left, rejecting Him, choosing sin: it's up to you.

# WORLD'S GREATEST SALESMAN

This great salesman talked with the woman at the well,
Told her of this thing so great, He did tell.
Salvation is free, given to all mankind.
The best in the world that anyone can find.

Wisdom had He, and knew just what to say.
His salvation is the very best way.
Teaching the people on Galilee's sand
Righteousness and God's salvation's plan.

And the wonderful product within His hand
Is fully guaranteed by His command.
Sufficient, paid-in-full for your very own use.
So, it is needless to say your reason or excuse.

He was convinced as a salesman should be,
That His precious salvation was needed by you and me.
Willingly He paid the price, took the shame of the cross
That you and I would not be lost.

Christ knows the "Customer," yes indeed,
Knows everything that you and I need.
Also, He understands our selfish way.
He knows we're just made from clay.

If turned away at the very first try,
Don't worry, He'll be back by and by.
Have you ever seen the salesman before?
If not, He may be knocking at your heart's door.

# IMPARTATIONS

# ABIDING UNDER THE
# SHADOW OF THE ALMIGHTY

The psalmist David knew distress and anxiety for many years as
Saul sought to take his life.
He poured out his heart to God,
Why stand thou afar off, O Lord, in this strife?
Why hide Yourself in time of trouble
as others use schemes they have devised,
As they boast of their heart's desire,
with cursing, deceit, and fraud, speaking lies.

The wicked, through pride, will not seek after God:
his tongue of mischief and pride.
His ways are always grievous, lurking in
secret places, waiting for the innocent far and wide.
He draws his net to catch the poor as he said in his heart,
God has forgotten, He's hid His face.
Arise, O Lord, lift up thine hand, forget not the humble,
show your servant your grace.

Wherefore does the wicked condemn God?
He hath said in his heart, Thou wilt not require.
Thou hast seen, for You behold mischief and spite,
to requite, deliver me from the mire
With thy hand: the poor commits himself unto Thee;
Thou art the helper of the fatherless.
Break Thou the arm of the wicked and the evil man,
we plead; seek out his wickedness.

The Lord hears the desire of the humble and prepares
their hearts and inclines an ear to hear
To judge the fatherless and oppressed, that the man of the
earth may no more cause fear.

Hide not Thy face from me in the day of my trouble;
hear me when I call; answer speedily.
O LORD, lead me in the right because of my enemies;
hear my prayer exceedingly.

David's prayer and worship continually in
good times and bad, caught God's all-seeing eye.
David inquired for reprieve of his enemies,
God save me, and the Lord heard his cry.
David learned to encourage himself seeing
God had revealed mightily His magnificent power.
The psalmist learned God was his rock, fortress,
and deliverer, and his strong tower.

Oh, see that the Lord is good, He goes before thee,
will not fail thee, neither be dismayed.
Fear not, my servant; behold, I will save thee,
and make you to be in rest, be not afraid.
I have redeemed thee, and have chosen you,
have called thee by name, thou art mine.
You are more valuable than many sparrows;
be glad, for the Lord will do great things in time.

Although battles and problems seemed to be on
every hand, David penned with assurance.
He had learned that God was his fortress and
 deliverer, a strong arm, a rock of endurance.
As he dwelt in the secret place, abiding under the
shadow of the Almighty as his stay,
He made the Lord a stronghold and his habitation,
regardless of what came his way.

# AS ONE

The many pieces of a puzzle can make one confused,
With so many shapes and sizes containing so many hues.
But in time and meticulous persistence, the puzzle is done.
The artist's work, his masterpiece, then becomes visible - as one.

The carpenter gathers his tools - wood, wallboard, and nails,
Adding to his list, hammer, a drill, and ruler for the details.
He works according to his blueprint while there is sun.
The architect's work of art comes together – as one.

Orchestras perform suitably with all instruments:
flutes, drums, and the oboe.
All are reading the score and practicing, each on the same flow.
When precise in its purpose for rhythm and tone,
then harmony is begun.
The conductor hears a beautiful symphony together – as one.

In John chapter 17, Jesus asks His father to set His children apart
From the world: they would live and believe from their heart.
Just as the Father thought, breathed,
and worked through His Son
Jesus was in His Father's will, working – as One.

The world doesn't know God; it's Him in us that they see.
So, when we are divided about God and His decree,
They receive mixed signals about God and His Son.
It's so important to pray and live in His love – as One.

I am not exactly like you, and you're not exactly like me.
Each of us needs to follow the plan that God wants us to be.
Each of our differences are fitting in our preparation,
For the Master's calling, worship and service – as one.

# BORROWED TOOLS

Elisha consented to the young prophets to build a larger abode.
So, they plighted themselves by clearing the grove.
It was during the long day's task
An anxious cry sounded, "Oh, no, alas."
The head of the axe sank deep in the lake.
How was one to explain this awful mistake?

When Elisha heard of the young man's disgrace
He broke off a branch and inquired of the place.
Then Elisha threw the branch where the iron had sank.
To the lad's amazement, the axe head floated to the bank.
Now the young man the borrowed tool could return,
And never forget the lesson he had learned.

Any task that God calls us to do,
He will furnish us with the tools to pursue.
We need never borrow or lean on another,
For God has a different work for our brother
So, pick up the tool that God has placed in your hand.
Just start at Calvary, where you'll see God's plan.

If you feel that you've tried your best and things aren't right,
Examine your heart, but don't give up the fight.
Maybe you've borrowed a tool instead of using your own.
So, press on and see what God has waiting for you at His throne.
We have a loving Father that knows that we're incomplete.
We can do all things through Him when we stay at His feet.

# BREAD IN THE MASTER'S HANDS

The Master was ministering to the
multitude about the kingdom plan
While His disciples were listening and learning close at hand.
Quite weary because of a long day and a crowd very large,
The disciples were perplexed at the Master's unrealistic charge.

"Assemble the people in groups, we can't send them away.
They faint without food, for they have been here all day."
The disciples searched and found a small lunch of fish and bread.
"Master, here is what we found, how can this many be fed?"

Jesus blessed and broke the lunch in pieces and gave the command.
"Go and put some food in each child's, woman's, and man's hand."
The disciples did accordingly, amazed at what had transpired,
At the impossible; Jesus fulfilled the hungry ones' desire.

We can be like the bread and be blessed with the Lord's power,
But we must be broken to be usable and
to be available for the hour.
For those who need encouragement and strength for the day,
We will be equipped for each of the souls that come our way.

God has given us the resources, if we will only learn to ask
Him to impart His anointing power for each imminent task.
We can give each person the bread of life, the gift of God's Son.
God can multiply our subservient efforts until the work is done.

# CHEESE AND CRACKERS

The Philistines stood on one mountain and
Israel on the other, a valley in between.
Each gathered for battle clothed with armor,
but nothing was happening on the scene.
Philistines' champion would taunt the
Israelites with his statue and scoffs.
This made the Israelites greatly dismayed
and afraid, so there was a standoff.

There arrives a lad that must not have
known the dangers of the battle.
Comes to the Israelite camp with all his
supplies and dismounts his saddle.
But David knew what he was doing, despite
his brother's indignation.
His father had sent him, answering all
the inquiries and harsh allegations.

Jesse had sent David with parched corn
bread for his brothers' nourishment.
And ten cheeses for the captains,
to convey his father's encouragement.
The older brother was angry at his
younger brother for his behavior.
Who was taking care of the sheep?
Questioning his misdemeanor.

The oldest brother was infuriated when
David offered to fight the giant.
Why did David come?  How could this
insignificant boy be this defiant?
Who was he that could do better than
 those trained in the trenches?

Who was he to give encouragement to?
This lad that plays in the ditches.

David's cheese and crackers were not good enough for his siblings,
Even though he followed his father's instruction and biddings.
Whatever he encountered to get essentials to the appointed place,
David showing up on the battlefield was an inexcusable disgrace.

Little did they know David's faith
and personal relationship with God.
It was just a fable about the lion and
the bear, thinking it a facade.
They were surprised by his simple way
in which he killed the enemy,
But it was what God had given him, to have the victory.

It is hard for the older brother to
accept the way of the younger generation.
They have different ways to present
the gospel to reach others for salvation.
We need to make sure what is said aligns with the Word.
The younger set can give the message in
a different way to be heard.

We need to be patient and mentor those that are aspiring to serve.
Their journey may not look like much
with only giving spiritual hors 'd oeuvres.
Cheese and crackers may have taken a
long time to study and prepare.
But with the mentoring of the older,
the spiritual meal given with care.

We each serve as we are assigned and
do our task to the best of our ability,

Giving a measure of leeway to
the younger careful, watching stability.
They will grow and mature as God leads them in their journey.
Our place is to encourage, watching for their souls for eternity.

# CRUMPLED UP PAPER

Crumpled up paper, to most, is seen as being
worthless, dysfunctional, and worthy of the trash.
Many people would agree with this statement,
but I am here to inform you of a newsflash.
This crumpled paper can become a swan, a novel,
a picture, or words written with great art.
Just because it's crushed doesn't mean that
it still can't be of use. It can be pulled apart.
A crumpled piece of paper can still
become a masterpiece,
with a little help from God.
Flatten out all the edges, smooth it out,
looking a little walked on and down trod.

We, like the crumpled paper, may have a
few rough spots with some lines and bumps
Seeming to stand out more than others,
hoping no one sees our inconsistencies and clumps.
But all of this gives us character;
it is part of God's unique plan as He has declared.
We still have hope and a future as
His plans unfold, as the prophet Jeremiah shared.
God knows whether or not this piece of paper
will become a novel, a poem, or paper mâché
This crumpled piece of paper will become
the masterpiece it was destined to be one day.

You may be a crumpled piece of paper
that has been crumpled and re-crumpled multiple times.
You had to find ways to pull yourself out of that trash can,
more than once making those climbs.
Trying and flattening out the rough spots
and smoothing the bumps and crinkles on your own,

You find that you can't do it, landing back in the trash can,
you have to go to God's throne.
We become more than conquerors through
Christ who loved us when we believe.
It's with Christ we can begin to be something
more beautiful than we could conceive.

You may not have put all these bumps and
ripples into this piece of paper all by yourself.
A rippled spot may be childhood abuse,
including neglect, homelessness, and stealth.
Molested as a child or an abusive marriage
or endured humiliation that put you on the floor.
Yet, there isn't anything that God can't fix.
He has the answer and will open the door.
These experiences helped to create the
character that is before you, His plan for fashion.
These experiences instilled hope, gratefulness,
resiliency, and compassion.

Yes, you may be crumpled, damaged with all that
you have been through in the conflict.
But remember, God said we are His workmanship
created unto good works; handpicked.
Some ripples come in waves while each connected
to each other in all directions.
Abuse, neglect, manipulation, and control, weaving in
and out, giving the wrong affections.
Abusive relationships make you question your judgement
and value, doubting your worth.
Remember you are more valuable than a sparrow that
flies through the earth.

God uses people that others think unlikely to
be that candidate for His Kingdom.

Noah, a drunk, Jacob was a liar, Leah ugly,
Gideon afraid, and Moses stuttered some.
Rahab was a prostitute, David an adulterer, Jonah ran
from God, and Job lost everything.
Matthew hated for his tax, Peter denied the Lord,
and Paul, the Christians did bring.
Zacchaeus was too little, and Naomi lost her
children and Martha was a pessimist.
So many people God used for His kingdom work.
This is just a small list.

It doesn't matter the trauma or baggage,
God can and will turn your life around.
Give you a new start, making you something
marvelous, with new life abound.
God will shape us into the kind of person
He wants us to be, a valued worth.
He created and set in motion a plan shaping
us for His purpose and work.
Jesus endured the cross, despising the shame,
and is set on God's right hand.
God loves and values us so much He sent
His son to redeem us was His plan.

We can look to Jesus the author and the
finisher of our faith for any trial.
God helps us deal with storms that arise
and stays with us all the while,
Telling us to cast our cares on Him,
trust and lean not to our own reason.
Rejoice in hope and be patient. God is in control;
He provides in His season.
Have faith in God, He will see you through;
He loves you and will never fail.
Praising God in the hard times brings victory
over every situation and gale.

Hold on to God no matter what happens;
He'll help you through that storm.
He will guide you into becoming a masterpiece
from the crumpled life to form.
It will take patience, prayer and reading the
Word to be used for greater appointing.
As God works through the ripple, bumps, and
crinkles and brings anointing,
God can take that crumpled mess and make a
beautiful, amazing masterpiece.
Just yield to His Spirit and He'll take you to
places and give you perfect peace.


Inspired by Pastor Jillian Kilburn

# DENTS IN MY ARMOR

When I joined God's military, He gave me armor shiny and new,
Along with His Word, instructing on its use and what to do.
It's been my salvation; without it there would be defeat,
But I have this armor covering me from my head to my feet.

I can do all things in Christ when I use my shield.
My faith gives me strength as I battle in the field.
God's righteousness helps me go in the direction I should,
With peace guiding my steps many times I've stood.

Don't judge my armor when you see dents here and there.
It just lets you know all the battles I have fared.
The testing of my armor has made me stand strong.
I can face another battle, knowing I won't go wrong.

By the word of my testimony and Blood of the Lamb,
I'm given the power to raise the banner for the Great I Am.
I may have a few bruises and dents in my armor, you see,
But I'm still armed and dangerous when God covers me.


Inspired by Pastor Sandra Jaime

# FOLLOW ME TO THE MOUNTAIN

We have seen many wonders the Lord has done,
but He calls his people near.
He longs to carry us on eagle's wings up close
for His people to hear.
He kept His covenant so the nations will know
of His love and grace.
He wants His people to come to the mountain,
to His holy place.

Before we can come near the place God abides,
we must cleanse ourselves.
Come humbly with reverence, bow down and
worship where God dwells.
When we come to the mountain,
we must not come without offering.
A sacrifice to show our love and appreciation
each should gladly bring.

It's at the mountain we find His righteousness
and just mighty hand.
He quenches the thirsty with a living water that
will satisfy the land.
A refuge is in His mountain, one can flee
from all one's enemies,
Because He preserves those that follows
His dictates and decrees

Righteousness will His people afford
in God's mountain with justice deep,
Giving prosperity to those who honor
His Word and commandments keep.
Staying close to the mountain, one
can hear and know His pure voice.

It's an amazing journey to abide in the
mountain, but it's a choice.

Not all will come to the mountain,
for the heart isn't right at the hour.
They don't desire a higher place in
God's kingdom or long for His power.
Our privilege in the mountain we find
the solitude and sweet rest.
It's a place where we can find all God's
goodness and be blessed.

It's when we allow God to escort us to
the mountain top's height
We realize the plans and blessings He has for us come to light.
Our understanding and faith begin to reach a greater elevation,
Seeing God's vision for what He wants for us in a new revelation.

So, follow me to the mountain to obtain what He has in store.
It's for those that have a hunger to know God all the more.
Follow me to the mountain for that new height of His realm.
With holy hands, pure heart to the
mountain wonders overwhelmed

# GET YOUR PRAYER THROUGH

Peter and his helpers toiled all the night with fishing nets.
The next morning Jesus asked if he had any fish yet.
Peter looked at the Master and sighed in despair.
But Jesus called "Launch a little deeper over there."

We have done that, nevertheless, whatever you say.
Willing to heed the Master's command, they obeyed.
The nets were filled and overflowed until they nearly broke.
It was then Peter realized it was because Jesus spoke.

After the catch was brought in and stored in its place.
Peter was in awe of the way the Master his troubles erased.
Sometimes we pray not receiving the answer to our request,
We feel that it is just his will to go through our trial as a test.

If we persevere and move heaven on our knees,
We will find that God's will meet our wants as well as needs.
There are times we need to launch deeper in his will,
To move the spiritual realm and his will to fulfill.

God may be working below the water level of His plan,
Working out things behind the scenes with his invisible hand.
So don't give up, pray until you get your breakthrough.
God is moving even if things don't go the way we want them to.
Don't give up until your help comes, whatever the need.
That "Net breaking blessing" comes to
those who stay on their knees.


Inspired by Bishop Dan Willis

# GET IT TO THE CROSS

There is power given to each child of God which we can use.
It's in the Holy Ghost's infilling, long ago God did introduce.
In the book of Acts told by Apostle Peter, verse 38, chapter two.
Today, it's still being poured out to all, to me and to you.

Like the batteries lying in a drawer, we have power to decide
Whether to utilize this source that God has allowed inside.
We can use this authority to become and accomplish God's desire,
Or we can let this power lay dormant, quenching His fire.

You shall receive power and be witnesses to every nation,
Is the command when we received this vital confirmation.
We become empowered by His authority, in His name,
His Spirit working in our lives, His sovereignty proclaim.

This spiritual authority can keep us when the road gets rough,
Giving us the strength when those challenges are extremely tough.
If we can get hold of the cross where Jesus' blood paid the price
We'll find His arms are strong and His covering more than suffice.

This spiritual authority ministers when
all falls short of consolation,
When we call on His name of which every
knee bows in every nation.
His death at the cross sealed His signature
for each blessing and need.
The Holy Spirit is ours for the asking;
we don't have to implore or plead.

This power will take you through trials
that seem hopeless and distressed.
When you find that place at the cross,
you'll feel wonderfully blessed.

# THE MASTER'S TOUCH

It changes your perspective on what is significant and genuine.
When trials are brought to the cross,
an unsurpassed peace you'll find.


Inspired by Bishop Dan Willis

# GET OUT OF THE BUSHES

David was requested to take food to his brothers in battle.
Hence, he packed the food, his carriage and horse did saddle.
As David gazed around a giant from Gath stood on the hill,
But David didn't see anyone of Israel, everything was still.

What is the meaning of this? Everyone is in hiding.
David thought a battle is where men were to be fighting.
"Go home." His brothers were angry with their sibling.
"This is no place for you," as they crouched trembling.

Are we not the children of God of the Most High?
After hearing the giant arrogantly Israel's army defy,
God has helped me slay the lion and the bear in the fold.
And this giant can be conquered that speaks so bold.

David went with his sling, a stone in the name of his Lord,
While the giant laughed at him, holding his spear and a sword.
The giant fell because David came out of hiding and took a stand.
God gave him the victory for the battle by His mighty hand.

Giants or tests cause us to hide among the bushes or trenches.
We have a mighty God who hears us as altars we make of benches.
There is a reward for winning, a freedom as we make a stand.
He gives the spoils of the battle and substance of the land.

Be encouraged, get out of the bushes, be strong in God's might.
We can win each of our battles and stand for what is right.
There is freedom from the chains of sin
when we walk in God's path.
Great are our rewards –
a life prevailing to conquer the giants of Gath.


Inspired by Pastor Frank Cruz

# HIDDEN SEASONS

A heavy-hearted king commanded
Daniel to be brought before his majesty.
It was never his intention to see
this arrangement; such a travesty.
Even as king, he could not change
the law once his decree had been set.
It was clear to him now his magistrate's
court had conjured this bet.

Knowing Daniel's character,
the way that he carried out his dictate,
He was the last person that he would have thought to humiliate.
The king, confident in Daniel's service
to his God and homeland,
Spoke and said to Daniel,
"Your God will deliver you by His hand."

A solemn night was spent in the
palace with no music or festivities.
Sleep was far from the king, pacing
the floor with anger and anxieties.
He most likely thought of the traits
that were in his servant over the years.
He was hoping the trust Daniel had in
his God was true, despite his fears.

The king arose early in the morning,
anxious to know of Daniel's fate.
He commanded the stone to be moved,
hoping the lions didn't take the bait.
He shouted with a lamentable voice,
"Daniel, was your God able to deliver you?"

"Oh King, live forever; because of my innocence, God has
brought me through."

King Darius commanded those
who conned him to have the same judgement,
Not only them, but their wives
and children received Daniel's punishment.
The Bible said their bones broke into
pieces as the lion mastered their cuisine.
The lions had waited at God's command
on which sustenance to convene.

Is that God whom we serve today
able despite what you've been through?
Despite cancer, public humiliation,
what they said, that divorce that tore you in two?
This lesson from Daniel will change your life; i
magine hearing in the den the roar of alarm.
Oh King live forever; God has sent angels and
shut the lions' mouths, there's no matter of harm.

The king was glad and delivered Daniel out of the pit;
Daniel believed in his God to the end.
When God finishes you, you won't look
like what you come through in your lion's den.
A little piece of you may die, but you won't be like you started;
don't fear the cruel.
God always has a way of making you come out on top and your
enemies your foot stool.

Daniel's accusers with all their family were cast
in the lions' den, eaten before they hit the floor.
Be careful what you say; God has a way of
flipping the script, settling the score.

Daniel's demise became the death of his accusers
because they hated his private life.
His critics could not find anything wrong with
Daniel's character, looking for strife.

When folks can't get you in your public life,
 they will start looking into your personal affairs.
Don't give them something to talk about;
let them find the same as Daniel, a spirit so rare.
They couldn't find anything in his public dealings,
so they dug into things that he did at home.
The only thing they could find was he prayed daily,
a ritual he did to his God alone.

They couldn't find anything publicly but his
prayer, so decreed for prayer only to the king.
The plan to boast the king knowing Daniel
would continue praying; his God was everything.
God moves, He moves with "suddenlies".
Be not weary in well doing in what you feel is right.
He has not forgotten you; when God arises, He arises,
and His enemies are scattered in plight.

Somebody has lied on you; before they hit the
floor God will avenge you of your situation.
A pagan king wrote unto all the people,
Peace be multiplied unto you, unto all nations.
If God can't find men of God to be a voice,
He'll take somebody that we least expect.
He will take the foolish things of this world
to get His Word across, His power to effect.

The king made a decree, men tremble before
Daniel's God, every dominion of His Kingdom.

The living God, steadfast forever, His Kingdom
shall not be destroyed and His dominion.
He delivers, rescues, and works signs and wonders
by the power of the God Daniel serves.
God used a pagan king to make His power known
and get the glory He deserves.

The end of the story is not looking up from the floor,
as you are knocked down with fears.
When God arises, you're going to be looking up;
praise Him from the floor through your tears.
After all you have been through, weeping endues for a night, but
the joy comes by the dawn. When God gets through, you will
prosper, but you have to stand still. It's God you're waiting on.

How you handle the hidden season of your
life determines how you handle your public matters.
What you do in your private prayer will determine
how you control yourself when life shatters.
Israel vacillated in serving God for 400 years and
had to experience God's judgment.
He tried to reach Israel with His tender kindness
and mercy before His punishment.

Before you point a finger, let me remind you God
always extends His hand of compassion.
He never lets judgment fall unless He has repeatedly
drawn them with some kind of action.
You think it was the first warning, but God sends a
grandmother or clerk at the grocery store.
He may use somebody in prison, a pastor, but He woos
His people with mercy many times more.

Babylon had come for the young, strong, and those
of the royal linage, in line for elevation.

Shadrack, Meshack, Abednego and Daniel were the perfect
candidates for Babylon captivation.
The devil is coming for you, your children, and
grandchildren; he's aware of whose you are.
You are a royal priesthood, a chosen generation,
a child of God, who loves you by far.

Grandmothers, praying does matter;
pray like you have never prayed beforehand.
The first thing Babylon did was change their names
when they brought them to the foreign land.
Daniel means "God is my judge" and they tried
to take his identity, hoping he would forget.
Taking him captive with a new pagan name,
hoping he would conform to the those he met.


Daniel looked in the mirror thinking, they are not going
to tell me who I am. He never altered.
I am the head and not the tail. I am above and not beneath.
I am the lender and not the defaulter.
I have been called out of darkness into a marvelous light,
a child of God striving for a crown.
When you know who you are, whatever they call you,
they can't strip you down.

The captors insisted the Hebrew boys conform
to Babylon meals to be fit to present to the king.
But Daniel requested he continue the covenant
with Israel's dietary laws only to bring.
Give us ten days void of the king's dainties,
meats, and wine and give us plain food instead.
The prince of the eunuchs replied, I fear the king;
you make me endanger my head.

The eunuch agreed for the ten days, allowing the Hebrew diet,
but after that you do it my way.
He brought them in front of the king after
the ten days and the king had this to say:
These young men look shining and younger,
and their countenance is so fair.
After an audience with the king, they were
considered far better than anyone there.

Daniel did not let his captivity change his
environment or how he served his God.
When you walk into your environment,
you are light in the darkness you trod.
He continued to pray three times a day in
his private chamber, to live how God expects,
So he could have the strength to handle the
public business with honor and circumspect.

When people say I am going to handle you
they are saying they have not prayed
But it is wiser to go before God and on your knees,
you should have stayed.
Prayer is the battle; go before God in prayer with
your armor and faith in His Word.
Then all you have to do is gather the spoils when
your prayer has been heard.

If you can't handle serving God when you
have a right to be offended,
You will not be able to handle public life when
people are open winded.
If you cannot stay still and keep serving,
you will struggle with public elevation,
So God will probably keep you on the
threshing floor until you come to oblation.

It's private prayer that gives one strength to endure
public humiliation, unmoved by excuses.
Where are the Esthers? if I perish, I perish.
Prayer is the ammunition the child of God uses
To make it through any decree that has seemed
to be appointed to our situation.
Wait on God; He will deliver and answer
your prayer, rewarding with great compensation.


Inspired by Bishop Dan Willis

# HOLES IN THE WALL

Saul sat on his throne with a javelin in his hand,
His heart filled with envy of David and God's plan.
David had to dodge the spears not once, but twice.
But God protected David from Saul's cruel device.

Saul sent David to command an army for demise.
But on his return, his victory gained honor in Israel's eyes.
God blessed everything David accomplished with great victory
Which made Saul hate David with boundless animosity.

David had a choice about how
he was to respond to all that he endured.
But he kept his heart right, his attitude humble and pure.
It's irrational how the king could be envious of a subordinate
And to think to the point of taking his life with hostile intent

When you are given lemons, you can choose to make lemonade
Or nurse your hurt, become hard hearted or have evil repaid.
But David continued to move up to be an armor bearer to king,
Doing what he was asked, while continuing to do the right thing.

It doesn't matter how you've been treated,
but the response you give.
God can make positive characteristics out of the negative.
He takes the struggles and makes our character as pure gold.
Regardless of what comes or goes, we know God is still in control.

All things work together to them
that are called according to God's will.
David had grace and anointing,
an assignment from God to fulfill.
A man of meekness, submissive, compliant despite life's troughs
Stood strong and victorious against the oncoming foes.

# THE MASTER'S TOUCH

David chose not to mourn the bad coming his way
No matter the hardship, slander or all who cried nay.
When God's hand is on your life, not everybody will celebrate
The special anointing but show their displeasure and hate.

You must decide to fit in where God has anointed you.
That assignment that makes you different, let it show through.
Special anointed first to become what God wants you to be,
With the grace and favor, a heart God longs to see.

You must walk in your anointing believing
God will do what He said.
Your belief has to be louder as you walk
as in your anointing lead.
David had power with God; Saul lost honor
although in the position.
A crown doesn't make you king,
but God's anointing gives provision.

Saul was envious of a lad so small, coming from a lowly place.
Saul had lost what he had, knowing David's future and grace.
It's in God presence the small become big in His mighty hand.
This was a threat to Saul, having lost the place in God's plan.

People are unhappy because they want what others have achieved.
What is yours is not mine and the load
or position unable to receive.
We go through the trials and warfare,
dodging all the darts.
The struggle makes one strong, creating
character and integrity in our hearts.

David was a shepherd, cleaning up after the sheep in the field.
He learned to fight the bear, lion, and the giant without a shield.
Satan will fight you when you are small in men's eyes.
He sees what is ahead for you in God's kingdom, a great prize.

David was in service to the king as the darts were thrown.
But David kept on playing his music; he was not alone,
Don't change your character or integrity due to Satan's scheme.
You are not less than what God made you to be;
you've been redeemed.

Pride cuts off people, hurt by others,
but don't let it change your aim.
Know who you are, remember as
His child He has chosen your name.
David learned to encourage himself as should we;
don't hang your head.
God has promised to never leave you or forsake you,
as His Word said.

Weeping may be in the midnight hour,
but morning brings great delight.
Encourage yourself; God is always on time.
Play your song through your fight;
Trouble doesn't last always.
Don't let the devil tear you down or take you out.
Don't let the enemy get in your music or
forget what your purpose is about.

David was faithful with the sheep,
not an overnight success.
There was a process getting to the place
where by God he could be blessed.
When Crowned king, David returned to the palace,
he could most likely see the holes in wall.
He remembered how God protected him and
the grace given through it all.

We may not be where God said we should be, but nevertheless,
God protects us, keeping us from the darts and all the stress.

We still may be broken, still sick, but God loves us where we are at.
God loves us in our mess. God will love in spite of any fact.

We can look back at David and see all the holes in the wall.
Holes made by the bullets, daggers and spears thrown at us all.
Holes seen and unseen –
those we didn't know God thwarted away.
Don't complain about the scars.  They tell the story of the day.

Scars God allows on us means we are still made it through.
God keeps the enemy at bay,
giving victory regardless of what others do.
Learn to celebrate others; when God blesses
someone else, do rejoice.
Pray for your enemies.  Bless them – a hard thing.
That must be our choice.

Be grateful for what you have,
be thankful for every hole in the wall.
God has brought you through
every trial and helped with every fall.
Let the holes in the wall remind us
how big God is if we stay meek.
He will take every wrong and make
us what He wants as His will we seek.


Inspired Senior Pastor Garland Mays, Jr.

# IT'S NOT WHAT IT LOOKS LIKE

The Lord spoke to Moses, saying the children of
Israel should camp by the Pi Hahiroth Sea
He warned Pharaoh would think he had the
upper hand, assured a trap the wilderness would be.
God would harden Pharaoh's heart, following them;
but God would get the glory in this fight.
Pharaoh, and all his host would know the power of
the God of Israel before the end of the night.

When it was made known the people fled,
the heart of Pharaoh and of his servants was adamant.
All the horses and chariots of Pharaoh and
his army overtook Israel's encampment.
When Pharaoh drew nigh, the children of
Israel lifted their eyes, and were sore afraid.
They began to expound on many of the dangers
and mistakes that this action had made.

Moses said unto the people, Fear ye not, stand still,
and see the salvation of the Lord this day.
God will shew His mighty power if they would
trust Him and His command obey.
The Lord shall fight for you and ye shall hold your peace,
your enemies shall be no more.
God was in control; they should make ready and see
what God had in store.

The angel of God, which went before the camp of Israel,
removed to the place behind.
Making the pillar of cloud go in front of the
enemy, their way they couldn't find.
In the morning watch the Lord look through the
pillar of fire and troubled the nemesis

# THE MASTER'S TOUCH

Losing their chariot wheels as they drove
them heavily causing great distress.

The children of Israel walked upon dry land amid the sea,
walls of water of great breadth.
Moses stretched his hand over the sea,
the water overtaking the Egyptians to their death.
The Lord saved Israel that day out of the hand of the Egyptians,
the enemy dead upon the shore.
God won the battle; as He had promised,
Israel would never see this enemy anymore.

As Moses spoke to Israel, seeing their enemies
no more, we must prophecy that today.
Put a death sentence on your enemies,
declare today is the day
You won't see them anymore, no more disease,
sickness, family strife.
Today is the day to declare the enemy has no
more control of your life.

The enemy watches you, not for good
but to find areas you are weak.
He doesn't want you to succeed in life;
your faults he'll always seek.
After Pharaoh let the children of Israel go,
he thought he'd had a judgment lapse.
But he rethought it; the wilderness was a trap, so he really had it
all in his grasp.

The enemy had them surrounded;
he was laughing, where is your God now?
If He is really real, give me the way
He is going to rescue you and how.
It's not what it looks like. It's a setup for you to go to a new level.
God will make your haters into elevators, despite the devil.

Elevate to the next level. There is a miracle in the making.
The devil wants to kill you, chasing you,
watching you drown, shaking.
We walk by faith, not by sight, even if it's
not the situation we choose.
The enemy is trying to get us to change,
but our faith we cannot lose.

The enemy will try his schemes, coming to kill, steal and destroy.
Our emotions, marriages and finances trying hard to employ.
But that's not the time to get out of our temptation or grumble.
We are comfortable until we must step out on faith, humble.

There's pain in the power; hold on, you will get through.
People of power have passed the test, won victories not a few.
They've overcome the enemy and sometimes you can't even tell.
They don't talk, walk like or even look like everybody else as well.

You can't get that power unless go through
instead of getting out of the fight.
Many are the afflictions of the righteous,
but God delivers out of all our plight.
People won't understand how you can praise
as the battles seem to never end.
Let me speak faith for those on spiritual life support,
speak the Word; that's power, my friend.

Going to the next level will cost you some
faith, money and even time.
Things you have to do are stay in the Word
and praise; no time to whine.
You may be going through for somebody
else as you give God the glory when done.
It's not what it looks like; it's a setup so you
have a testimony of the victory won.

It was a trap not for God's people, but for the enemy
as God looks on the circumstances.
We may cry and struggle in the dilemma, but God
is using this to expose your enemy's advances.
Those who go through the battle are the ones that
God looks on and with His power covers
As six hundred chariots, 600 captains and pharaoh
at large overwhelming adversary hovers.

Everything gone on the front, 400 years of slavery
and nothing to fight the foe.
But remember, no weapon formed against you shall prosper.
You got God. Just know.
No artillery – no kind of strategy and the
enemy on the bank, what do you do?
You may hear the enemy behind you.
Just know God is for you,  you can make it through.

Others may think it crazy; you'll never make it.
The Lord is looking, but not at you.
He is watching each, personally, planning to
confuse the enemy as he tries to pursue.
Making the enemy angry with each other,
taking their wheels off, driving them away.
Just remember, God is working on this and the
enemy will dearly pay.

The enemy wants us frustrated, thinking why go
to church, why persevere?
But God will make the enemy turn on each other,
their hearts plagued with fear.
God is working; step aside. God gives permanent victory;
the enemy won't come back.
Go through the struggle, speak to the situation.
Remember God's promises are not slack.

It's not what it looks like; no, it's not a trap.
God has the enemy where He wants them.
Deliverance is in the same place as trouble begins;
have faith even though things look dim.
There is something God requires us to do.
Lift your hands and praise. Thank Him for the win.
This confuses the devil. God is taking the wheels off;
watch the ways He will defend.

When God sets you free, you will be free indeed,
A testimony may have taken you years
But He will use you to help someone else, which will
strengthen them and quiet fears.
It's not what it looks like. We must learn to trust God
and give Him the praise.
Watch your enemy fall into the trap never to see the
rest of their days.


Inspired by Senior Pastor Garland Mays, Jr.

# LAY ASIDE YOUR GARMENTS

The hour of Jesus' greatest test was still before Him;
His mission was clear.
His love for His disciples was His concern,
for His departure was near.
The weight of the world and the salvation of
mankind was a heavy sentiment.
Despite the immensity of His assignment,
He laid aside His garment.

There were more instructions and truths that
He wanted them to embrace,
So He laid aside His own pangs to serve
His disciples in a special place.
As He dined and instructed those that
He had spent several years,
He put away His own feelings to serve
and quiet the disciples' fears.

That He would go away and would
come again didn't make sense to some.
Questions arose and He'd answer each as the
enquiries would come.
These were the men He had invested
His love and kingdom truths.
His goal was to have them equipped for the
future and attitudes.

Even in His heaviness of what was ahead,
He served the ones He treasured.
Planning the meal, instructions,
all was an importance He measured.
Despite what He was about to go through in a few hours,
He laid aside His heaviness, He His followers' lives empowers.

This is an example for a Christian in the way we should live.
Despite what we are going through, there is more to give.
We have to lay aside hurt or anger, not with an attitude of chagrin.
Do what we are called, or we find our good become sin.

There are many garments we could be wearing for an excuse,
Hindering one from the appointed Master's use.
We allow bad relations, heartaches or too busy to care,
Encumber the heart to others service to share.

We are to follow what Jesus exhibited,
putting His own difficulty aside
In His darkest hour and a service
that He would to others provide.
Let us put aside what hinders and so
easily besets us from our mission,
But be steadfast in that we are called
and live out His commission.

# LEAD ME OUT OF BETHSAIDA

The people stood in front of Jesus with great anticipation.
They had brought a blind man for a merciful consideration.
Jesus took compassion on the man and took him by the hand,
Bidding His bystanders to not follow Him and the man.

Once they were out of Bethsaida, to make spittle was His decision,
Then applied the mud to the man's eyes and inquired of his vision.
Things were not clear; men around him looked like moving trees.
Thus, Jesus once again put the homemade salve so he could see.

Jesus completed the task and bid the man to go his way,
But not to go back to Bethsaida, nor a word to convey.
Bethsaida would not accept the mighty works Jesus had done.
There was no repentance; the town rejected God's Son.

Bethsaida means "house of fish," being a desert place,
Void of compassion or desire, a city that was abase,
A city that Jesus did not want to work another wonder
In the bounds of people that demeaned His work asunder.

God often brings the blind out of the darkness they are in
So He can work His wonders, not where there is sin.
A healing for spiritual vision comes when the Spirit is free
Of all the hindrances of doubting and hypocrisy.

It's so important, the kind of company we keep around.
We tend to lose our spiritual vision where sin is found.
We need to go before the throne for a supernatural perception,
Be anointed with His salve keeping our visual perfection.

God counsels me to make me gold tried by fire,
And clothes me in white raiment, the purest attire,
So that the shame of my nakedness does not appear
And anoints my eyes with salve; also makes me to hear.

# THE MASTER'S TOUCH

The Spirit of the Lord comes upon me to speak with diligence,
To heal the brokenhearted, bring to the captives deliverance.
Recovering of sight to the blind that need spiritual views,
And to set at liberty them that hurt and are bruised.

Don't let me stay in Bethsaida, that unworthy desert place,
But hunger for Your Word and long to seek Your face.
Lead me from the surroundings that make me blind,
But take thy hand and apply that salve so divine.

# MARK THE PLACE

Naomi was reaching old age and was
concerned for her daughter-in-law, Ruth.
Ruth needed a life of her own, and Naomi
had to face the inevitable truth.
She made a bold decision that changed the
course of both their lives,
Giving Ruth an unconventional command on
which many a generation thrives

Requesting Ruth to go to the threshing
floor as Boaz scattered the grain,
Ruth was to approach him for a greater
request that seemed a little insane.
"You are his next of kin and he can take care
of you much better than I,
So make yourself presentable, simple and plain,
go to him and explain why."

Ruth attended the threshing as she had
done before, but lingered until twilight.
As instructed, she waited until Boaz had
eaten and drunk for the night.
She quietly positioned herself at the
place where Naomi had wisely coached.
Ruth was to make sure she had presented
herself with the right approach.

At midnight Boaz woke startled,
and noticed her at his feet with great trepidation.
"Who are you?" he questioned as he turned,
fearing personal condemnation.
She identified herself there at his feet,
covered with a portion of his shroud,

Explaining she was his handmaiden and
giving her reason; this was allowed.

Boaz assured her he would do all that
was required by law of the land.
But there was someone else closer and
was next in line could have her hand.
Boaz bade her to stay where she was and
not go until she had safety of day.
Then she went back to Naomi excited,
waiting for the verdict to convey.

When it was all said and done,
Boaz redeemed Ruth as his bride and very own,
Making their union a path for
generations' salvation to be shown.
It was at the place marked where
Naomi had requested Ruth to be positioned
Brought Ruth great and mighty blessings that came to fruition.

We need to mark the place at the
feet of Jesus for our needs and desires.
But it's the approach and our faith that
God always of us requires.
We can stand on His Word and know
that He will always come through,
Staying in the place where He can show
us what He really can do.

We may have to stay the night until His
light filters our way.,
Sometimes seeming to be alone, but in
the end, He has the last say.
Mark the place; that's where you'll
find the anointing and rest.

We can be assured and comforted;
God has stood the test.

Let your spiritual vision see what God has in store,
Whether it's a promotion, greater ministry, or winning a war.
Mark the place of victory, a grander faith or vastly goal.
Everywhere we place our feet, His power will never toll.
Mark the place, lay aside every weight.
Stand on His promises; God is never late.
Mark the place of the vision God has given you.
He'll go to great lengths – see now what God can do.

# NOTHING BE LOST

Jesus taught and healed the great multitude on the Galilee shore.
The people followed Him when
they saw His miracles all the more.
Then Jesus went up into a mountain
with His disciples as the multitude trailed behind.
As it was getting up in the day, Jesus felt the people needed to dine.

He lifted His eyes and saw the great company
that needed nourishment for the day.
He said to Philip, "Where shall we buy bread?"
as they could not send the people away.
Philip was overwhelmed, answered Him,
"Two hundred pennies worth of bread
Would in no way provide for all the people
needing to be fed."

But Jesus was not moved with Philip's lack of faith unconcealed,
Despite what worries or concerns the disciples revealed.
One of his disciples, Andrew, Simon Peter's brother,
had searched the mass.
"There is a lad with five barley loaves,
and two small fishes: but that will not last."

Jesus said, "Make the people sit down"
even though the number was immense.
Jesus took the loaves, break the bread,
gave thanks, then gave the command to dispense.
When they were filled, He said,
"Gather up the fragments that remain, that nothing be wasted."
Twelve baskets were gathered that remained over
and above the bread that had been tasted.

When times are hard and resources low,
needs are not being met in our lives,
It's the time we are careful and frugal
with what we have; every penny scrutinize.
Prudently we use each spare dime,
making sure not to waste anything in our hand,
Taking the time to the best of our ability
thinking through with a frugal plan.

But as we are blessed with miracles and
see the amazing things the Lord provides
Standing in awe we forget how to handle
the overflow correctly in His eyes.
We tend to waste the extra blessings,
forgetting to apply each choice wisely,
Instead of making sure the surplus is used
with vigilance, just as precisely.

Jesus was teaching His disciples to be
accountable for each of our blessings, great or small.
Whatever is put in our hands is what
we are responsible for, whatever befall,
We are to use wisdom with our resources,
whether financial, intangible, sometimes minuscule.
Making sure we have used each of them to
the best of our ability as a God-given tool.

# OUT OF ORDER

Jesus came to the man who lay at the
pool an inordinate length of time.
It was an encounter that would change
his life, blowing his mind.
We have our ups and downs in life;
we see the good and the evil,
Often experiencing the possibility
of trouble, making life's upheaval.
Even if you have to cry your way to victory, no matter the fight,
No matter how you get it, get it.  Give it all your might!

Can we trust God when we're in trouble for 38 years?
Struggling and giving it what we've got, through our tears.
Whether sick or homeless, in pain,
business relationships are spoiled,
The man dealt a long time with trouble,
but he continually toiled.
Does anyone care about your struggle
and the length you must wait?
You can spend time, but you can't save it.
It's up to you to keep the faith.

Time talks to you, asking,
"Where is God in your troubled place?
Everyone is getting blessed while my issues are never are erased."
It's coming.  Your turn's coming.
You will reap if you don't grow weary.
Did not God say He would do a new thing –
make a way in the contrary?
Midnight is only 60 seconds long and joy comes at dawn.

We must hold on and know that God
has a way no matter how long.

He makes a river in the dry place and fountains for the thirsty
He has all in control even if we can't see His unlimited strategy.
Jesus came to the man, blocking his
path to get what he thought was his solution.
He could not see who was in front of him;
his mind didn't come to the conclusion.
In front of him was the great I Am,
the alpha-omega, the Everlasting One.
King of kings, the healer, who takes
the problem, through whom victory's won.

The man saw the protocol of the pool,
thinking it would change his circumstance.
His faith was attached to the pool and not to
any other avenue of chance.
There is latitude of means that He will
find a way to get our attention,
Using eccentric methods as we hang on to
our protocol of church tradition.
The Lord wants to do whatever it takes to lift
the limits off you
To trust Him with our troubles; He is our
answer to make it through.

The man almost missed his healing because
his faith was in what he knew,
Looking to experience of the past, not seeing
the miracle in another avenue.
Don't let your faith run out. Faith is what carries you through.
You never know when it's coming. Never give up, whatever you do.

Everything was the same, but it was the
day for this man's transformation.
What happened? Jesus came -
defying the religious protocol reverberation.

The man kept coming to the pool,
kept giving all that he could give.

Let the devil know I'm still serving God;
I'm not dying, I'm going to to live.
We must keep moving through divorce, pain, and stress,
Keep going despite bankruptcy, wounds, keep going in our mess.
If you don't move, you die; keep moving, make up your mind.
Keep pressing; it's faith that moves you to the front of line.

While waiting on the water,
your Star-Trek anointing, or marriage abyss,
Wait on your favor, keep the faith,
so your victory you don't miss.
Jesus asked the man what he wanted as
he humbled himself before the Lord.
Our posture determines our promotion
and favor that God can afford.
Dogs put on electronic leashes,
to keep them continually confined,
Eventually can be unleashed,
due to the conditioning of their mind.

The devil put a leash on our minds,
then it's bondage, becoming a stronghold.
What is in the mind becomes behavior
which is passed to our children enfold.
We get comfortable in our bondage,
adapting to the life of captivity.
Never let the consistency of bondage
cloud your sights for your victory.
Rise up and take your bed and walk, never to use it again.
Let Jesus speak to your situation whatever your pain.

Bringing to life those dormant possibilities inside of you,

Let Him flip the script so you have a complete breakthrough.
Pick up excuse or whatever has you comfortable in your distress.
Tap into the power inside you. Pick up your mess.
Pick up your mat to make no provisions for you to return.
Burn your bridges, doors are closed no more to yearn.

How serious are you? I'm not going back; make it a resolution.
Make a right now decision to walk, never to live in confusion.
Midnight only lasts 60 seconds; weeping may endure for the night.
Joy comes in the morning when we don't give up the fight.
It doesn't matter your status,
whether you are big or small or qualified.
God calls the undeserved so that no flesh can boast, but He will
be glorified.

God takes you front of line –
skipping steps that go beyond rational precision.
Don't be disappointed when some
think you don't look the part in your new position.
Even amid brethren or enemies,
don't be ashamed of your anointing.
God is a God of order, but when it's
your turn God disrupts the appointing.
God focuses on the humble and faithful
pressing through the night long.
He takes things out of order and gives
victory over things going wrong.

John 5:1-9
Inspired by Senior Pastor Garland Mays, Jr.

# OUT OF TURN

David would talk to his sheep and
play his harp in the field each day.
To most he seemed to be a loner,
but that was his time to worship and pray.
This lad's heart was toward God;
that put him in a special place in God's eyes.
David was unnoticed by the family,
so to be chosen for king was a total surprise.

David had no idea for the protocol
guiding the people he was to rule.
He was used to talking to animals
 and a simple sling was his fighting tool.
His attire was rugged and he had not
seen too much other than his herd.
His speech was simple, and personality
may have been somewhat reserved.

Saul was rejected by God; his soul was
tormented as time went along.
So his servants thought music would
help so had someone play him a song
David's talent gave him a place in the
palace to soothe the tormented soul.
But this was the avenue for David,
as in his life God took control.

Going to the palace was way out of
David's comfort zone, way out of place.
Now the door was shut on his childhood ways,
now a new life staring him in the face.
With the door behind him and a new direction
that he didn't have any idea how to go,

God put a friend in Jonathan to guide him to his destiny, a great
comrade in the know.

David had a friend that had connections,
in sight of the palace and the kingdom,
Someone that had his back and reassured
him of his rights and then some.
Jonathan gave David his own royal robe, sword,
his girdle, and his bow.
Giving him the ins and outs of protocol for the
new position as he needed to know.

David, from the tribe of Judah, not one who should be king.
God's favor was on David, and it was an out of the ordinary thing.
David was now in line for the throne,
but it wasn't the normal etiquette.
David's obedience and faith put him
in a place that God wanted him set.

So, when your gift puts you in a new and uncomfortable position,
And the door of the past closes and
you are anxious about the intention,
That is when one should trust God as
He shuts one door and opens a new.
He will provide the means and guidance that is needed for you.

He will provide the people and the
connections that He so divinely provides
To be right there and reassure of your place;
a friend that positively confides.
When God puts you in your uncomfortable place,
just be confident.
As He shuts the door on the old,
He gives you the directions prerequisite.

We need to be willing to step
through the doors that God has revealed
And be willing to keep the doors He has shut forever sealed.
God shuts and opens doors to get us where He wants us to be.
Know the open doors are His way our rite of passage sees.


Inspired by Senior Pastor Garland Mays, Jr.

# RESTING IN THE WEARIED PLACE

It wasn't the most welcome place to rest, on the well's edge of
hardened clay.
The journey had made Jesus tired
even though it was only noon day.
He sent the disciples away for food as the sun was hot and
scorched His weary frame,
Finding himself in Sychar, the place called
"drunken, falsehood," representing shame.

Though He was tired and exhausted,
He talked and graced the woman's thought.
There was a thirsty soul needing living
water trying to comprehend what was taught.
The disciple came upon His conversation
and wondered why He would regale a reprobate,
Knowing the long history of dissention of the
Jews and Samaritans; how could He relate?

One can minister, becoming weary
doing what is required for all the tasks,
Find themselves extremely tired thinking
the next step will be the last
But wherever one finds a place to rest,
God puts us in the least likely place.
We just need to know when to fall on
our knees and seek His face.

Rest if you must, but there is a journey that needs to be finished.
God is our refuge; in His presence our strength can be replenished.
Some will not understand the purpose
or perseverance ministry entails,
Not having the same calling will sincerely offer decisions of derails.

God bids you come to Him who labor and heavy laden,
and He will give you rest.
For our work is not in vain as we find that
hiding place that gives us strength in our test.
He is our shadow in the cleft of the rock and
restores as we wait on His grace.
He gives rest from all your enemies,
making you dwell in a safe place.

The Lord shall give you rest from thy sorrow
and bondage wherein you were made to serve.
Take His yoke upon you and learn He is meek
and gives the rest His servant deserves.
The rest may be in a place that we think
uncomfortable or inopportune,
But God will restore the weary soul in your ministry,
 even at high noon.

# MY ROCK

I stand on the rock, my strength, my solace,
a strong dwelling place,
Leading me through that great and terrible,
whatever I must face,
Wherein were the fiery serpents, scorpions, or drought.
The rock is my source where the water springs out.

The rock covers me in the cleft, affording a protective nest.
His work is perfect and His ways where truth does rest.
In Him is no iniquity, assuredly just and righteous is He,
Puts me on the high places so I surely can see.

There is honey in the rock and oil that feeds and heals,
Brings fatness to all those their lives one does yields.
One can build an altar on this rock and find grace
To bow and worship before the Lord in the special place.

One can find salvation, the rock can be their constant stay,
In the great fortress, deliver, and keep the enemy at bay.
He brings showers of blessings in the mountains so steep,
An unfaltering shelter, a steadfast tower He does keep.

He is my rock of salvation, my buckler, hides me in the storm.
The secret of His tabernacle, safe in His arms, secure and warm.
I cried to the Rock, be not silent as I seem to go down in grief.
He bowed down His ear to me and speedily came to my relief.

He brought me up also out of a horrible pit, out of the miry clay,
Set my feet upon the rock and established my goings, so I can stay.
Therefore, for Thy name's sake lead me,
and guide my pathway pure.
Be Thou my strong habitation,
whereunto I may continually endure.

The LORD liveth; and blessed be my Rock;
let God be lifted high.
O come, let us sing unto the LORD:
let's reverence Him, magnify.
Let us make a joyful noise to the
Rock of our salvation most excellent.
Enter the Rock, and hide in His love,
honoring Him fitly reverent.

# SUPPOSING JESUS

The feast of the Passover was an event
for the whole family to attend.
Now the yearly feast and all its festivities
were coming to an end.
After a day into their homeward journey
Mary and Joseph became aware
That Jesus not with them or in the crowd,
giving His earthly parents a scare.

Returning, they found Him in the
temple among the teachers and scribes,
Astounding those around Him with his
questions that left them surprised.
His mother said unto Him,
"Son, why hast thou thus dealt with us?"
Jesus answered her with words that
struck her heart and quieted her fuss.

Today we are still supposing He is lost
during all of our earthly distraction.
Then it takes us more time to back-track,
finding His will, trying to get back into action.
Our agenda and ideas are good until we
forget to ask Him His will and plans.
It is so important to keep the Lord in our
Father's business honoring what He commands.

When we are obedient and make His
will treasure of our heart and soul,
We will grow in wisdom as we live our lives;
His blessing will unfold.
God will elevate us as we attend to all things
of heavenly dominion.

Nothing can stop what He has for us;
criticism, jealousy, or opinion.

God's favor comes because of the nature
of the depth of one's emotion,
A heart that pants after God and gives
Him praise with a consecrated devotion,
An approval which is beyond our fondest
expectations or thought,
A position or honor is greater than
anything that can be bought.

This favor spills over into our journey here on this terrain,
Allowing one to find the indulgence we never thought to attain.
A grateful heart and vigilant attention to what God wants us to do
Will help us to never be in a position supposing Jesus is there too.

# THE INTIMATE PLACE

God loved His creation, talking with Adam in the cool of the day.
It was His pleasure to have divinity and humanity relate this way.
He made a beautiful garden where He and man could fellowship,
In this place where He had design for His creation to be equipped

Then one day God was looking for Adam for their evening chat,
Calling out, "Adam, where art thou?"
He was not where he usually sat.
Adam was hiding because he was afraid;
he had made the wrong choice.
Hence their relationship was estranged,
but God could hear his voice.

Adam took leaves to cover himself,
but the leaves failed their purpose.
The leaves dried up and crumbled,
revealing real sin on the surface.
God took an animal and sacrificed
its life to conceal Adam's disgrace,
Shedding the blood so they could resume,
and a relationship embrace.

We find ourselves in hiding and afraid
because of our broken rapport,
No longer eager to commune with
God or enter His presence as before,
Trying to cover up our sin with leaves
so no one will notice debauchery.
It's only when we bring our brokenness
to the Lord that we find recovery.

The Children of Israel had the tabernacle
to meet and worship God in

He gave all rules of what animal to sacrifice to cover their sin.
God was still looking for intimacy
with His creation as He had in Eden.
This was not really God's ideal way,
but was temporary, just for a season.

God sent His Son to bring a closer
intimacy between God and man.
Jesus had a relationship with His
disciples as He walked Earth's sand.
Jesus taught them a more powerful relationship to descend.
A Comforter would give power and strength,
closer than a friend.

With the Comforter, greater things shall ye do as He dwells in you
Gives you power to overcome, our help in all things we need to do.
In Him we move and have our being, t
his greatest intimacy with God.
This intimacy, God's pleasure,
as man travels this earthly sod.

We know we have intimacy with
God when we worship regardless who's near,
Or care what someone's wearing or worrying
about tomorrow's fear.
Knowing the battle's not ours, giving
strength, guidance, and direction
This Comforter makes intercession for our
needs and understands our affections.

God is still saying "Adam, where art thou,"
a bond with man continually ensuring.
Mankind has tried to find countless
ways to shield his sinful wrongdoing,

Ways that delude away from the wrong,
but don't redeem him to the throne.
God had to send His Son to redeem man,
to redeem back mankind for His own.

Man needed the shed blood to cover the sin,
the restoring intimacy's price
So He sent His Son, shedding His blood;
intimacy was gained with great sacrifice
God loves His creation and longs for a
relationship daily devoted and genuine.
He takes pleasure in His children worshiping
Him as we were designed.

# THERE IS BLESSING UNDER THE DEBT

Life seems chaotic, with so much suffering
we don't know which way to turn.
Our anger and hurt are clouding our thoughts,
causing our hearts to burn.
But if we will turn it over, giving it to God,
He will help us to forget.
We find the blessing of forgiveness under
all of the heavy debt.

We have tried to walk in God's will, His statutes tried to yield.
In all of our trying, doing the best we can, we seem a failure still.
Guilt takes hold of our hearts and we beat ourselves up and fret.
But God has the cleansing power to free us of the debt.

God is gracious when we follow foolish, pretentious avenues.
Gently prodding us with His hand, while we turn away His woos.
Sometimes He allows us to fall on our face left there to set,
Washing away the pride, finding His grace under all the debt.

We are faced with trials seemingly overwhelming and oversize,
Anxious, agonizing over the mountain standing before our eyes.
Unbelief clouds our spiritual vision, and we soon forget.
It's through faith and trust God will help us overcome the debt.

The innermost parts of our hearts are important to be cleansed
Daily with God's amazing mercy, His love removing our sins.
It is the greatest grace that will help us never to forget.
There is a blessing, whatever it may be, under the debt.


Inspired by Pastor Vera Tucker

# THERE'S SOMETHING ABOUT OUR CRY

You have been crying lately, needing something in your life.
You have made the wrong choices: the hurt has caused strife.
Blinded by the tears, you can't find the right direction.
Feeling alone, the only thing you're sure of is rejection.
But just remember, there is hope; God is touched by our tears.
He is the refuge and fortress through all our fears.

Hagar, the bondwoman, and her son were sent away
With no home or family, just bread and water for the day.
She went a little way from the lad and began to cry.
It was going to be hard to see her son slowly die.
But God provided a well for them to be revived,
Promised to make of them a great nation; they survived.

Jabez was a challenge to others in his day and time.
But his prayer was that God would in his heart find.
The Lord would bless him and enlarge his borders,
That God would keep him from evil and spoilers.
Jabez longed so much to cause no more anguish,
God granted his prayer in the midst of his languish.

The blind beggar by the road cried as Jesus passed by.
The people tried to quiet him as Jesus drew nigh.
"Jesus, thou son of David, have mercy on me."
He grew louder; he wanted Jesus to hear his plea.
"What wilt thou that I shall do unto thee?"
"Oh, that I might with my eyes You see."

Just as each of these had a dilemma in their life,
There is an answer to the multitudes of strife.
We have a high priest who knows our humiliations.
Through it all, we can find in Him our propitiation.
Come into His presence with your worship; come nigh
To God, there's something about your cry.

Inspired by Pastor Frank Cruz

# THROW AWAY THE CUP

The lame man was sat at the Beautiful Gate for all to behold.
There he remained until his eyelids and hands he did fold.
Daily he shook the cup put in his hand, asking for compassion,
Needing to be delivered from his incapacitated cessation.

Little did he know what this day would bring as he settled in,
For two men came to the gate to enter the temple within.
He held out his cup, "Alms, alms, please, just a few."
But the men who stood before him said, "We have none for you.

Silver and gold have we none," Peter and John did proclaim,
"But such as we have, arise and walk, in Jesus' name."
Immediately the lame man received strength in his crippled feet,
Jumped up and ran, praising God through the city street.

There are some that sit at the Beautiful Gate holding their tin.
At their gate of Beautiful transition – not too far and yet not in.
Just outside of the place where God wants to do His will,
They just need a hand of deliverance their lives to fulfill.

We sit and hold our cups, asking for minute needs for our lives,
When He wants us to lay down the cup and silence our cries.
Enter the temple beyond the gate
with expectancy and confidence,
Believing no matter what the fetter
for an anointing power of deliverance.

# WHAT MEAN THESE STONES?

The day had come for Joshua to replace his mentor and friend.
God had command Moses to anoint and tutor him to this end.
Challenges lay ahead for which Joshua was groomed and prepared.
He now heard directly from God, as his predecessor had shared.
"Moses, my servant, is dead;
now therefore arise, over Jordan ensue.
Thou, and all this people, unto the
land given to them, that will I do.

"Every place that the sole of your foot shall tread,
That have I given unto you, as unto Moses I have said.
From the wilderness, this Lebanon, even unto the great Euphrates,
All the land toward the going down of the sun, unto the great sea.
Be strong and of a good courage:
for unto this people shalt thou divide
The inheritance, the land, which
I swore unto their fathers did confide.

"My law shall not depart out of thy mouth,
but thou shalt meditate day and night,
That you observe to do according to all
that is written therein: to do right.
Then thou shalt make thy way prosperous,
and thou shalt have good success.
Follow all that I command you,
then you shall be blessed.
Be strong and of good courage, be not afraid,
neither be dismayed.
For the Lord thy God will be with you wherever you go,
give rest and shade."

Joshua arose and charged the people to prepare for the excursion,
Encouraging them to forge a new
journey regardless of the diversion.
The people all packed and ready for
the passage of the Jordan's terrain
An experience imprinted in their minds,
an event to be told again and again.
As they marched through uncharted
ground by each tribe a stone was to be selected
For a memorial at the end of their journey to be erected.

These stones were not an altar for
prayer but a monument of remembrance
How God had made a way,
had kept them and given them deliverance
Joshua named this place Gilgal, meaning
"a place of circle or wheel,"
For God now had rolled off the children
of Israel the curse of slavery's ill
For forty years they carried the stigma of
Egypt's deep tears
God had desired to heal and restore His
people for many years.

This charge still holds for the believer as we journey,
each as we walk in our purpose,
His law in our mouth night and day,
to observe deep in our hearts, not on the surface.
Our successes and victories are reliant on
our obedience to His mandates.
Strength and courage are a must,
a steadfast duty of His law and dictates.
One can be assured He is our fortress
in everything we are called to achieve
As we stand strong in His might and choose to believe.

If you have not yet come to God, in Egypt's curse and despair,
Or you have found yourself wandering
in the wilderness not knowing where
Your life is going to take you with no purpose you can find,
Cross over your Jordan, where God is longing your life to design,
Lift the burden of sin and give you a new lease on your life.
Come to Gilgal where God will roll away all sin and strife.

You also can make that monument
as a testimony of what God has done.
It may not be stones, but another
thing that will remind you and everyone.
No more wandering in the wilderness
with many years of guilt and shame
But a wonderful deliverance that comes
from trusting in Jesus' name.
Then you will have a reminder of that
miracle that was given to you..
As a result, you have the testimony to
tell of what God can do.

# WHAT'S MY NAME?

There's a fight going on you can't see with the natural eye:
it's in one's spirit and mind,
A spiritual battle for self-worth being
fought regarding one's identity and place to find.
Though concealed in a secret place,
the ramifications manifest in one's actions or talk,
Questioning who I am, which can only be answered
by examining what their past has taught.

Regardless of where you are in your spiritual walk,
we are all sinners saved by grace.
That means the playing field is level,
no big "I" or little "you," all starting at the same place.
All have as filthy rags for righteousness a
nd need the saving power of the blood of the Lamb.
It is necessary to look at one's maturity in Him daily
to stay focused on who I really am.

In the Bible days Jabez prayed, asking God to
bless him indeed and enlarge his territory.
"Oh, that Your hand would be with me,
keep me from evil causing pain," was his life's story.
A name was not just something you picked from
a basketball player or favorite TV star,
It was a prophecy over that child's life,
and this name had significance of who they are.

A name was not given by his enemies,
nor friends, but his family living in the same household.
Folks on your job don't bother you
nothing like when your family is disrespectful and cold.
This brings a level of pain that creates
control on how you live the rest of your life.

One learns to cope with things spoken over them,
a stronghold becoming an inner strife.

Conversations and attitudes are influential to
those living in however dysfunctional a family,
What actions or words done at home mold the
children for success or calamity
Mom may not like men because of a divorce or
being mistreated by a person with difficulties.
Dad may think the job is not good enough,
but it still puts food on the table and pays utilities.

Dad may have complained about his job
every day when he came home in the evening.
So, the child is unable to work, saying people
at the job are no good, so now you're leaving.
Never mind you were late three days, but it's like Mom said,
men are no good, that's my boss.
But Jabez's prayer was not for abundance,
but to break a generational curse, feeling lost.

No one is perfect, we're all trying to do the
best we can to find our true identity.
The first thing is to break the generational curses
to free us to go further than our family.
This means going further than what we are exposed to,
seeing beyond our circumstances.
The challenge is to subdue and take control of a stronghold;
with God's help, take those chances.

A stronghold means to fortify through the idea
of holding safely in own's mind and heart.
Weapons of our warfare are not carnal,
but mighty through God pulling down those fiery darts,

Casting down imaginations and every
high thing that exalts itself against the Word,
But bring into captivity every thought in obedience, readiness
of submission of what is heard.

Reactions are symptoms of strongholds, and these
strongholds can keep things in or out.
It keeps one living in a box based off their own
experiences; anything different causes doubt.
People will tell you how far to go based on their
own experience, for that's all they understand.
But God has much more for you than you can
even think or imagine; follow His plan.

Some people don't mean harm nor are envious,
but they can't see beyond their compass.
But Jabez had another ear which gave him hope
and an expected potential bonus.
He heard "I'm more than a conqueror, a chosen
generation, and a royal priesthood."
Sometimes you must let people know when they
say the wrong name; listen to the good.

Strongholds are mind-sets that need to be torn down
and let go of our self-esteem.
We carry the trash bags tending to only see images
in a wrong mirror's scream.
We put on fancy clothes, and shop at Nordstrom
for new lashes, new shoes, and socks.
This is clutter. It's uncomfortable to walk in
freedom because it's easier to stay in the box.

Snap at somebody you don't like, it' easier to
have an attitude and let a heaviness loom.

Don't want to be bothered, go through stress on a job,
when home send children to their room.
 Strongholds are designed to keep things out
and to keep you locked in, barriers all around.
What we don't realize is that we are keeping
ourselves in bondage, but freedom can be found.

Strongholds never go away when you are older;
an angry boy becomes an angry man.
It just stays in our comfortable place and
becomes a bigger issue out of hand.
A bitter little girl only becomes a bitter woman;
bullies never change no matter the age.
Forty years later you try to manipulate and intimidate –
becoming a bitter rage.

What power does the past really have?
It festers and guilt begins you can't ignore.
The Devil wants you to ignore what you've been
through, but it will only happen some more.
He wants to you repress issues, so you won't deal
with the problems and find peace.
But he who confesses brings repentance,
obtaining mercy and freedom, sweet release.

Left undone, our strongholds will bring regrets
as we often sweep those sins under the rug,
Which will reduce one down to that one mistake
everyone remembers – don't shrug!
The past will have you live in either fear of the
future or regret of things in the past.
Strongholds will stay until we confess and the
power of the blood - hold fast.

Strongholds can reduce you,
then you have become no more than a slave.
Moses had a speech impediment,
Jacob, a liar, but we are not defined by how we behave.
It's good to embrace strengths and
weaknesses, only an indication of our potential.
But one thing we need to do is forget what
lies behind and strive for greater spiritual.

We must learn what God says about us and
what plans He has appointed for us to do.
He gives full life in empty places and well-watered
gardens, gurgling springs that renew,
Rebuilds the rubble foundations, restores old ruins,
and makes communities livable again,
Gives redemption and freedom;
there's no condemnation when He takes all the pain.

His Word says all things God work for the good
of those who love Him, who walk in His path,
In all these things we are more than conquerors
through Him who loved us, free from wrath.
We're convinced that neither death nor life can
conquer us through Jesus' mighty power,
Giving us the mercy and grace to overcome
strongholds previously that our minds did devour.

One needs to embrace God's sovereign
ability to work good from all of life's sin,
Recognize the difference between disposition
shaped by past and determine to win.
By God's help, set those wrongs to right through
confession of our wrongs and forgive.
Let God's grace silence our shame, change our mindset;
in victory newness live.

Neither height nor depth, nor any creature,
will be able to separate us from God's love.
Old things have passed away; all things have
become new through the Savior above.
When you figure out who you are,
it will be manifested as your destiny you obey.
It is not something you create as
God has already planned, knowing the way.

In Genesis 32:24 Jacob was left alone
and wrestled a man, but neither prevailed.
So, the man touched Jacob's thigh out of joint,
but Jacob his intensity hailed.
He said, "Let me go." But Jacob said,
"I will not let thee go, except you bless me."
And he asked Jacob, "What is your name?"
And he said, "Jacob." His day for change of destiny.

Instead of a deceiver, a liar or cheat, Jacob was Israel,
a man of many nations,
A prince and power with God and men,
called of his children for many generations.
Jacob called the place Penial, for he had seen
God face to face and his life preserved,
A new outlook on the future as he faced the
greatest test in his life less perturbed.

The difference between Jabez and Jacob:
Jacob lived up to his name.
He tricked his brother and own father
 for the birthright, causing his shame.
Jacob was now living in abundance,
living his best life, but still in repression.
Could not get free until he surrendered
to God with humble confession.

Stuff does not define who you are.
What you got, where you've been, or credentials hold
You will never be fulfilled trying to keep up with the Joneses;
everything that glitters is not gold.
We define success with things that can steal our identities,
sneak up from behind as success.
It's whatever validates us, makes us feel significant,
finally attaining those beloved quests.

We spend money, we don't have to buy things we don't need
To impress people we don't know and we don't like nor heed.
God wants us to know what true success is, which will free us
From the deceptiveness of pursuit chasing this worldly fuss.

Failure is to succeed at something that really doesn't matter,
Spending our whole life climbing the corporate ladder
Then realize it was leaning against the wrong wall.
What is your motivator has become your downfall.

Ecclesiastes 4:4 tells us the biggest motivator
is envy, like chasing the wind.
Worshiping is what seems to be the goal,
 but what is it in the end?
God gave us ten commandments,
two of which He said not to bow.
This will have a punishment for idolatry
for generations if we allow.

Something that we think worthwhile –
chasing after the image of success –
The more that we allow it to drive us,
 the more it consumes our quests.
It becomes a place for all our energy,
our time and our assets.

The name is called worship.
If it not toward God, idolatry threats.

Jacob found himself alone and had spent quality time with God.
Jesus even did this in the Garden and Moses
atop the mountain's sod.
Jacob sent his family to the other side,
for a time of soul examination.
His separation was a time for genuinely
searching for his soul's sanctification.
God's justification brings transformation,
but we can't hear God, there's too many distractions.
We must work, answer the phone, watch the news on TV,
and follow all the world's attractions.
God will start a fight with you right where you are,
will get in your comfortable place.
But loves you too much to leave you there;
He will get in your business, face to face.

Your destiny will never be comfortable,
but God's desire is for us to grow and be complete.
The goal of a wrestling match is to get one to submit,
comfort will keep one in defeat.
The moment in the fight that changes your course
will transform the rest of your days.
At that point we must rely on God, follow
His commandments and learn His ways.

Pain is not always from your enemy;
pain brings change and some gain.
It makes you pay attention to threats against your body,
correction to obtain.
Jacob went from fighting with God to holding
on and would not let go.

His place of separation and consecration
brought blessings of conquering his foe.

Speak the truth about yourself based on
what is said in His Word; God loves you.
Until you are at peace you will not have
a relationship that is true.
Know who you are and whose you are,
for your best days are in front of your journey.
Stand up in the ring and shout your name
while you defeat the enemy.

What's my name? What does God say?
I'm His chosen, a royal priesthood and special child.
I am the head and not the tail, more than
a conqueror and power over the Devil's wile.
I serve a God whose name is above
every name in heaven and earth.
He is Alpha and Omega, Prince of Peace,
 King of Kings; that confirms all my worth.


Inspired by Senior Pastor Garland Mays, Jr.

# THE DISH TOWEL

A new dish towel! You hang for all to see.
You're glad to add to your towel family.
Gratefully you use it every day.
It's there when dishes are to finish.
Never let its duties diminish.

Easy to grab if the pan is too hot.
Toss down on the table at the spot.
For spills it's the one you'd pick
Because it's durable and thick.
Wet the end to wash a little chin.
That's when you notice it's a mite thin.

Company's coming! Hurry replaces it in a jiffy.
The new one you think is pretty and nifty.
The old one is stained and a bit torn.
We can't let the company see one worn.
We'll use the old again as soon as they go.
And hope the flaws of your kitchen they never know.

# THE KING HAS NEED OF YOU

King David summoned his servant and
inquired of Jonathan's family generation,
Because of Jonathan's and his covenant,
David wanted to show his consideration.
Ziba, the king's servant, replied and revealed
Jonathan's lame son living in Lodabar.
Due to the trying to escape in war,
had left this man destitute and scarred.

Ziba, the king's servant, went to Lodabar to
fetch Mephibosheth as the king had decreed,
Explaining to Mephibosheth the king had
need of him because he was Jonathan's seed.
Mephibosheth bowed and wondered why the
king would have an audience with such destitution.
But the King looked beyond his needs and carried
 out the purpose of his friend's restitution.

King David invited Mephibosheth to feast
with him at his table and royal lineage,
Restored unto him all his father's land to s
ustain him and his fields to replenish.
David sent Ziba and his servants to till the
land and gather the harvest of each field,
But it was up to Mephibosheth to be the steward
of what the king had restored and its yield.

We are summoned by our Heavenly King to sit at
His table and enjoy His kingdom.
Like Mephibosheth, living in Lodabar,
a place of shame, and fallen, we still can come.
The King looks beyond our needs and restores
what seems impossible and never could be,

If we will heed His calling regardless
of our situations and our inadequacy.

King Jesus is waiting with outstretched
arms to give what is impossible with men.
Removing shame, wiping away tears and
lingering guilt that is within.
He makes us His child along with all the
benefits offered by His unending grace,
Allowing us to be stewards and sitting us
before Hs table where you and I have a place.

# THE MASTER OF NEED

God made the sea; it needed water creatures that swam with ease.
The sky needed the birds to soar so stately in the tranquil breeze.
He made the sun, but darkness needed
the moon and stars at night.
He made man who He made needing
Him to be His heart's delight.

There is a need in all our lives that differs in so many ways.
We may have hunger, hurt, or find our way in all the haze.
He puts in the capacity that we need something to be filled.
We need to trust Him to make it happen, our paths to yield.

Pride gets in the way, which is one of God's displeasures,
Hindering one to ask God to do the miracles beyond measures.
Our perception of our need keeps us from receiving our miracle.
We must believe God is greater than the
need that makes us hysterical.

God promised Elijah that He would sustain him until it rained.
It looked irrational; God instructed
Elijah to ask a widow to sustain
The barrel of the widow was just enough
as she obeyed Elijah's command.
Day by day the oil and flour were supplied
as she immersed her hand.

We are looking for God to make our need go away wholly.
But He is teaching us to trust Him
for our daily bread, on Him solely.
God takes those that have need to
help those who are in like position.
Each can give what they have and
together things come to fruition.

God gives in many different measures
when taking care of our deficiency.
The grace may come in overflow or
one increment at a time proficiently.
Put your need in the hands of the
Master who can handle your worry.
Let go of your pride and ask Him
for the grace to show His great glory.

Printed in the USA
CPSIA information can be obtained
at www.ICGtesting.com
LVHW010622090924
790326LV00013B/427